SEA **FISHING**

The complete guide to angling from your boat or kayak

SEA **FISHING**

The complete guide to angling from your boat or kayak

JIM WHIPPY

ADLARD COLES

LONDON • OXFORD • NEW YORK • NEW DELHI • SYDNEY

ADLARD COLES
Bloomsbury Publishing Plc
50 Bedford Square, London, WC1B 3DP, UK
Bloomsbury Publishing Ireland Limited,
29 Earlsfort Terrace, Dublin 2, D02 AY28, Ireland

BLOOMSBURY, ADLARD COLES and the Adlard Coles logo are trademarks
of Bloomsbury Publishing Plc

First published in Great Britain 2010
Second edition published 2013
This edition published 2026

A catalogue record for this book is available from the British Library

Library of Congress Cataloguing-in-Publication data has been applied for

ISBN: PB: 978-1-3994-3072-2; ePub: 978-1-3994-3071-5; ePDF: 978-1-3994-3073-9

2 4 6 8 10 9 7 5 3 1

Typeset in Proxima Nova Light by Lee-May Lim
Printed and bound in China by RR Donnelley Asia Printing Solutions Limited

To find out more about our authors and books visit www.bloomsbury.com
and sign up for our newsletters
For product safety related questions contact productsafety@bloomsbury.com

CONTENTS

INTRODUCTION

This book provides a few ideas on how to catch fish for people who are not skilled in sea angling. It's aimed at those who sail, cruise or just spend time on the water around the coast of the British Isles.

The weekend sailor will often see mackerel shoaling or a bass rising and wonder, 'How could I catch a few for dinner?' There's nothing better than a bit of fresh fish straight from the sea and in this book the author uses clear pictures and instructions to show you how to make a catch. The book is intended as a guide to show how to catch fish while cruising along, drifting or peacefully at anchor, because different methods are required for each. There are numerous pictures showing clearly which fish are likely to be caught so they can be identified easily. We have also included sections on what you can catch as you travel further afield and how to prepare the fish for cooking, with some suitable recipes for use on board using limited ingredients and utensils.

Rods can be kept on board with feathers on, in case a shoal of mackerel is spotted on the surface. They can then be swiftly dropped over the side and hopefully catch a few fish while they are still in the area. For other species the tackle will require some slight changes that we will guide you through.

For the absolute beginner we explain the basic tackle required and move on to show how to get the best out of each item and when it should be used. We cover in a step-by-step format a few knots that are most commonly used by boat anglers and give a rundown on baits and how to present them to the fish. In each section of the book we identify the likely species that will be caught using that particular method and warn if any of them need careful handling due to sharp spines, fins or teeth.

The first method of fishing we look at is trolling because this is by far the easiest way to catch something as the fish generally hook themselves, and the boat can continue its journey while you are fishing. Trolling is generally carried out with the rod secured in a rod holder and left there until a fish takes the lure and starts the rachet going as it takes off line. Lures can be a set of six mackerel feathers or a single lure or spinner and, providing a suitable weight is used to keep it working just under the surface, the fish will do the rest.

We then show how to fish on the drift with the baits being pulled across or near the bottom. Drifting can be very rewarding as baits can be employed that will attract a wider range of fish than are found by exclusively trolling. If the ground is very rocky a paternoster rig, with hooks suspended off the bottom, will work best and keep tackle losses down to a minimum. Over sandy ground or gravel a flowing trace with a hook on the bottom is best for flatfish and several other species.

Then we explain how rewarding fishing at anchor can be, especially for the larger species of fish. At the end of a day's sailing or cruising, with the anchor securely down, it's fun to put a rod with a decent sized bait over the side to see what you can catch. In a strong tide, the tackle needs a suitably-sized lead weight to hold the bottom and allow the fish to find the bait.

Fishing from a boat doesn't require a lot of expensive equipment or high levels of skill to start with, but once you catch the bug you will be hooked for life and will want to find out more about the subject. This book will hopefully encourage you to expand your knowledge and try different methods of angling, alternative baits and find out more about the different fish we identify in each section.

In this edition we have added a chapter on kayak fishing, which has taken off in a big way over the past few years in the UK. Being a cheap way of getting afloat, with no berthing or marina fees, it allows the angler a chance to fish marks bigger boats can't get to. There is also a new feature on ground bait and more about using beads.

WHAT DO I NEED?
A quick guide to get you started

GETTING STARTED

Anyone who regularly goes afloat – whether in a motor cruiser, dinghy, yacht or kayak – will have seen evidence of fish jumping or shoaling on the surface and maybe wondered how to catch them. Showing how to do this is exactly what we want to achieve with this book, without too much technical jargon and fancy expensive equipment.

A wide range of sea fish can be caught using basic and inexpensive tackle if you follow the simple instructions. Fish are not difficult to catch provided you use the right methods at the right time for each particular species. What this book will give you is the basic knowledge about the feeding habits of fish, their favourite habitat and how to catch them, calling on the shared experiences of professional anglers.

To start with, the very minimum equipment is a rod, reel, set of feathers and a lead weight. With this very basic setup it is possible to catch at least ten different species: mackerel, scad, garfish, pollack, bass, gurnard, pout, coalfish, codling and whiting. They won't all be caught on the same day or in the same area, but during a season's fishing this is the potential.

Tackle shops are full of different rods, but what are they all for? We look at which rods are required for someone starting out and when to use them. It's the same with reels, the choice is sometimes overwhelming, but in fact there are really only two basic types – the fixed spool reel and the multiplier. One reasonably priced multiplier and a cheap fixed spool reel will suffice for all the methods shown in this book.

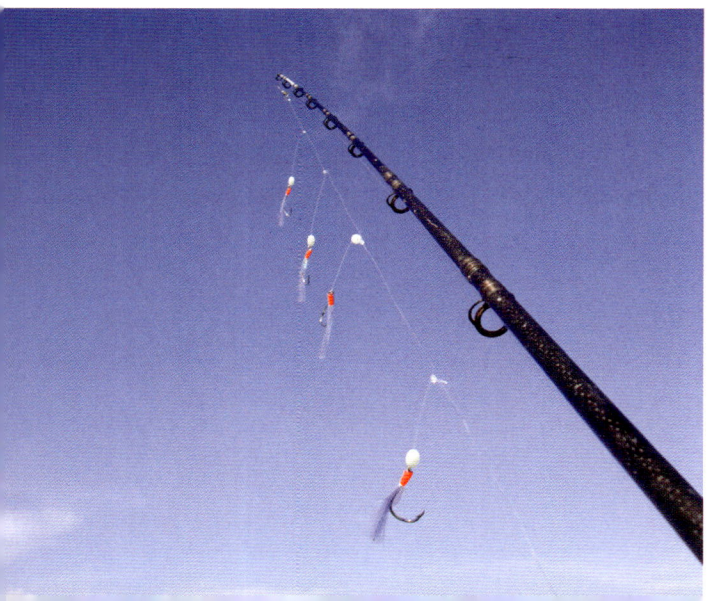

← The most basic method – a set of feathers.

TERMINOLOGY

The names of the equipment, tackle and fishing methods can be confusing so here is a simple explanation of some that may crop up when discussing sea angling.

Trolling	Pulling a lure behind a moving boat.
Gilling	Working an artificial eel on a long flowing trace.
Downtiding	Fishing from an anchored boat with the line over the stern.
Uptiding	Casting tackle with a grapnel lead uptide from an anchored boat.
Main line	The line on the reel.
Trace	The line that holds the hooks.
Flowing trace	A flowing trace is one fished on the bottom of the seabed below the weight, while a trace is either referred to as 'up the line' or a paternoster rig.
Paternoster	A trace with hooks suspended above the weight.
Clutch	The drag setting on the reel that allows the line to be pulled off.
Tubi or running booms	A device that holds the weight and allows the line to run through.

RODS
MULTIPLIER ROD

A multiplier rod is one set up to take a multiplier reel. This means it doesn't have a large bottom ring like the fixed spool rod because the line comes off a multiplier reel fairly straight. A fixed spool reel lets line off differently and needs a large bottom ring to allow the line to run through easily.

It really doesn't matter too much what rod you use as any old rod will catch fish. The most important item will always be the right bait or lure. What I can advise is which style of rod will be easiest to work with, and you need to get as close to this suggestion as possible depending on how much time you intend to spend fishing.

Boat rods are not expensive and one between 2m and 2.5m in length, with a fairly soft tip, would be ideal. These rods are very robust and will take the knocks if they are shoved down in the hold with all the other things that accumulate on a boat. The more expensive rods are lighter and will be more enjoyable to use, but are not vital at this stage. If looking in your local tackle shop for one, ask for a 15/20lb class multiplier rod, as this will be ideal for most styles of fishing we will cover. This rod will be used while the boat is on the move, or at anchor in deep water and strong tides.

FIXED SPOOL REELS AND MULTI-TIP RODS

Apart from the multiplier rod and reel, it would be handy to have a fixed spool reel, combined with a multi-tip rod, for all the occasions when a lighter setup is required.

As storage is limited on boats, the multi-tip rod will cover the need for having several rods on board. The rods are suppled with either twc or three tip sections that can be quickly changed from a regular tip to a lighter one in minutes. The lighter rods with the fixed spool reels are easy to use and can be cast to any fish seen near the boat. Being lightweight with a soft tip section, they make fishing more fun as the fish such as mackerel and bream will give a good account of themselves.

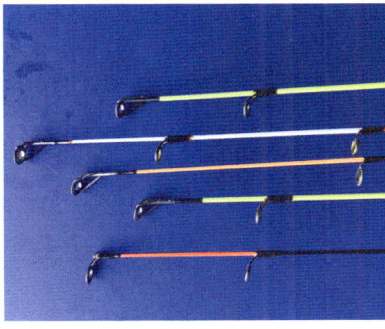

↑ Fixed spool reel.

↑ Multi-tips.

← Multiplier reels sit on top.

TOP TIP

A good rod and reel combo is important. To begin with it should balance near the reel – you want to fight the fish not the rod!

REELS

MULTIPLIER REEL

The multiplier reel sits on top of the rod and is set up to be used right-handed. There are a few left-handed multipliers on the market but they are not widely available. When casting with a multiplier reel the line needs controlling with the thumb and this can take some practice. For use while trolling or bottom fishing, where casting is not required, they come into their own as they are much better at handling heavy weights and big fish.

Some small- to medium-sized multiplier reels can be purchased quite reasonably, but the better quality ones can cost a lot more. The multiplier reel should be filled with 20lb nylon (mono) line – this is a single fibre line that comes in a range of colours that can be used depending on conditions.

   I don't advise using braided line for the occasional angler, as nylon is much more robust and lasts longer. However, see page 23 for more information on this type of line.

⬆ Bulk spools containing nylon (mono) line.

⬅ Muliplier reels are fixed on the top of the rod.

FIXED SPOOL REELS

The fixed spool reel is the cheapest and easiest to use and should be matched to a longer rod, with a large bottom ring, that allows the line to flow off easily when casting.

A fixed spool reel (below) is straightforward as you can flick the line out by pulling back the bale arm and holding the line with your forefinger. The line doesn't need to be controlled during the cast and the bale arm clicks back into position when the reel handle is turned. A fixed spool sits below the rod with the handle on the left.

Most reels allow for the handle to be switched over if winding left-handed proves difficult. The fixed spool reel should be filled with 12lb or 15lb mono line.

The bale arm of a fixed spool reel winds on the line in a criss-cross action that is ideal so the line doesn't bury itself.

Fixed spools can be used left- or right-handed and hang beneath the rod. ⇒

THE FIXED SPOOL REEL

The fixed spool reel is becoming more commonplace on boats as it offers trouble-free operation and is built to last. The one pictured here has been adapted for right-handed use.

SETTING THE CLUTCH ON A FIXED SPOOL REEL

The clutch on a fixed spool reel can be adjusted either at the front of the reel...

...or right at the back.

It should be loosened so that line can be pulled off with a firm steady pull.

THE MULTIPLIER REEL

Multiplier reels have a gearing that means every rotation of the handle turns the spool round two or three times. This multiplies the amount of line retrieved per turn of the handle making it more efficient winding in the line.

The multiplier reel is used on the top of the rod while the fixed spool ree and the older centre pin reels are hung below the rod. Most multipliers have a star drag on the side that can be adjusted to allow the line to be pulled off if a big fish takes. Some of the more expensive reels have a lever drag. This can be set to the correct tension so that when the lever drag is pushed forward to the strike position it's always at the right tension. If more tension is required, the lever drag can be overridden by depressing the stop button and pushing the lever further forward.

SETTING THE CLUTCH ON A MULTIPLIER REEL

The clutch can be set by adjusting the star drag on the side of the multiplier reel.

The lever drag multiplier reels have a drag setting that can be preset to the required tension.

BASIC TACKLE

The following items will give you a good start for sea fishing and other, more technical, items can always be added later:

- Swivel link or connector
- Lures
- Plastic tubi booms/running legers
- Zip sliders
- Beads
- Spools of nylon
- Hooks
- Weights
- Floats

Firstly, you need a type of swivel link or connector for the end of the line. This makes it easy to clip on lures or feathers and change them quickly if required. The type of lures required will be discussed on pages 26–31.

For bottom fishing (catching fish on the seabed) at anchor, a running leger or tubi boom needs to be threaded on to the main line. These are bent plastic tubes that allow the main line to run through with a swivel link on the bend of the tube to take a lead weight.

A packet of multi-coloured beads is useful for adding above the hooks to act as an attractor for flatfish. Putting on a bead between the boom and the swivel prevents the swivel jamming in the tube.

A spool of 20lb nylon (mono) for making up traces and a few packets of hooks from size 1 to 4/0 will cover all the basic fishing methods. A range of lead weights from 2oz to 1lb will be required to get the tackle down to the fish and a couple of floats for the fish that swim in mid water.

← Some of the basic tackle needed, such as tubi booms, swivel links and hooks.

Tackle shop dealers can be a wealth of information on local hot spots and current catches, and are only too eager to impart their knowledge and advice to anyone who is prepared to ask for their help.

SWIVEL LINKS

On the end of your main line – that's the line on your reel – you will need a connection so that the end tackle can be put on easily. The end tackle is the trace and hooks that will ultimately catch the fish. As it's quite likely that during a fishing session the rigs will need to be changed, instead of tying and untying all the time, it pays to put on a swivel link. This is a swivel that rotates to prevent line twist and breakages, with a clip that is opened for the line to be attached. There are several types of swivel link; one of the neatest is the American Snap Swivel.

⬆ Gemini speed links with a swivel make changing rigs easy.

⬆ The American Snap Swivel is popular and easy to use.

The silver swivel link shown below has a return on the clip that stops it pulling out. The Gemini speed clip, shown on the previous page, is another well known brand used by many match anglers as it can be changed quickly. A swivel with a clip is used to connect lures, traces and booms that may need to be changed quickly during a fishing session. A plain swivel (without a clip) is neater and is used in a trace that doesn't need to be taken apart whilst fishing. Of the bigger fish, the conger eel can spin like a top as it nears the surface and will break quite heavy lines if swivels aren't used.

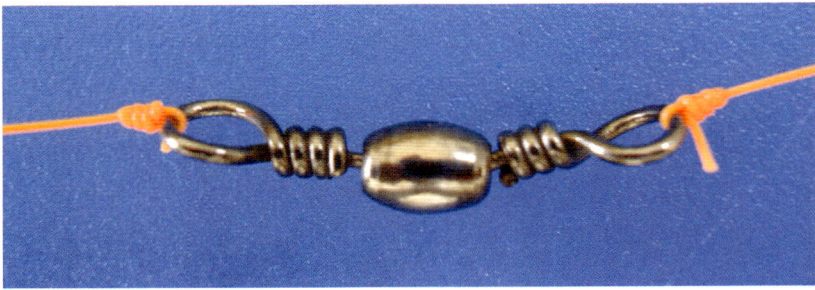

⬆ A plain swivel used on a trace will prevent line twist.

⬆ Weight connector on a tubi boom.

⬆ The swivel link here has a return on the clip making it very reliable.

 **TOP TIP**   Use a plain swivel to prevent line twist, breakages and tangling.

RUNNING BOOMS

A wide array of booms are used in sea fishing, all aimed at keeping the line from tangling as it is dropped to the bottom. They are also used so the fish can pull on the bait without feeling the weight of the lead.

The most widely used are plastic tubi booms that are inexpensive, but do the job. The line is threaded through the tube, then a bead is slid on before a swivel link is tied on the end. The weight is clipped on to a lead link that is fixed in place where the tube bends.

There are heavy booms made from thick plastic for fishing deep water, where large leads may be needed, down to short lightweight ones for playing about with small fish in very little tide. One handy version of a sliding boom is the zip slider. It is very short, but doesn't often tangle, and works best with a single hook trace of around 1.5m in length.

A fixed wire boom can be used when fishing with bait a few feet off the bottom for bream and whiting. Although plastic booms are the most popular, if you know when and where to use wire booms they can improve your catch.

↑ Running booms of varying sizes can be used for anything from dabs to conger eels.

BEADS

A packet or two of beads in a mixture of colours can be used in several ways when sea fishing from boats. Plaice are particularly drawn to some coloured beads on the trace, just above the hook. Two colour combos that are very popular are black and green, and black and yellow. The plaice will follow the bait when drifted along the seabed, even biting at the beads as well as the bait. Sequins can be used to good effect if placed between each bead as they are slid on to the trace, adding more glitter to the rig. Luminous beads can improve catches if fishing in low light or darkness. Floating beads can be used to keep the bait just clear of the bottom and wave enticingly in the tide, making it more noticeable to bottom feeding fish.

A rubber bead can be threaded on to the main line before the end swivel is connected, as it prevents damage to the top rod ring if the line is wound up too far or too quickly. This often happens if a youngster or an inexperienced angler gets excited, for example when a shoal of mackerel is first located. The rubber bead acts as a cushion and prevents damage to the top eye.

⬆ Plaice are extremely attracted to beads.

 **TOP TIP** If you are fishing in low light, or water with low visibility, try some luminous beads — these will help attract a catch.

MAIN LINE

One of the biggest changes in the sea fishing world is the widespread use of braid instead of mono (nylon) for the main line on fishing reels. It has some big advantages over mono, such as the lack of stretch, but it's not so abrasive resistant. Braid is expensive compared to a bulk spool of mono but can be a lot more fun to use as the bites are much more positive.

✔ FOR BRAID

Firstly, braid has virtually no stretch in it which means every little pull on the line and every bump over the seabed is felt through the rod. Bites from small fish are magnified and this can be a big advantage. On the downside it means the line is often pulled in too quickly before the fish has got the bait properly. Braid is also thinner than nylon so less weight can be used in a tide as there's less resistance. Because braid is thinner than nylon and extremely strong in comparison it pays to stick to at least 30lb breaking strain.

✘ AGAINST BRAID

Because braid is made from soft woven fibre it is not as resistant to abrasion as nylon. If it rubs against a wreck or rock, or catches on a boulder while drifting it is much more likely to break than even the cheapest nylon. This means it is best to have a few metres of nylon leader when using braid so it can take the knocks and bumps. The leader can also act as a buffer when winding in a decent fish by absorbing the head banging or sharp pulls. With plain braid on the reel every pull will be felt on the rod tip and if the rod is too stiff it can result in the hook pulling free. Knots are another hazard: braid tends to slip, so simple knots like a blood knot will come undone.

These spools of braid are far more expensive than nylon but have certain advantages. ➡

DEEP WATER

Because braid is absorbent it can be coloured during manufacture, like the line on this large multiplier reel. The line is a different colour every 10 metres, which can show the angler the fish's depth when fishing deep water. By watching which colour was on the reel when the fish was caught, the bait or lure can be let down to the same depth again.

⬆ Multi-coloured braid can indicate the depth the fish are feeding at.

TIDY TACKLE

Keeping your bits and pieces of tackle somewhere you can find them easily requires a bit of organisation. A small tackle box is needed to keep all the bigger items in, including the reel, lead weights, knife and hand wipes.

While a rig wallet will be handy for floats, beads and swivels they are used less for rigs. These are now wound on plastic spools that are much easier to use than pushing them loose into a rig wallet, especially for multi hook rigs. The spools are safer to use as the hooks can be pushed into the plastic and unwound in sequence with less chance of a tangle. Even a set of six mackerel feathers are easy to have on a spool, as they will always find a way to get into tangles as they are unpacked from their packaging.

⬆ Fishing rigs wound round plastic spools.

⬅ A sturdy tackle box can double as a convenient seat.

 **TOP TIP** Keep your traces on spools so they do not get tangled.

TYPES OF LURE

FEATHERS

A swivel link needs to be tied on the end of the main line so that lures can be clipped on and changed easily. The first lures to try are ones commonly known as feathers, although they generally aren't actual feathers nowadays. They can be made of all sorts of man-made materials.

Some of the popular ones such as silver shrimp, hokkai and mini-shrimp consist of four to six lures with a loop at the top to connect to your main line and a lead link at the bottom to connect to your weight. Some don't have the lead link so you will need to add a swivel link or something similar for your weight.

The next big question is how heavy a weight should be used? It depends on the speed the boat will be going but generally 6, 8 or 10 ounces will get the lures under the surface enough to work. After letting out between 30 and 60 metres of line, watch the angle of the line to see that it's running down sufficiently to pull the lures along below the surface. Also look back to where the lures are, and if you see them skipping along the surface you will need to either add some weight or slow the boat a little. Feathers can be used from an anchored boat by working them up and down. Change depth regularly until you locate them.

SINGLE LURE

Switching from a string of feathers to a single lure means another slight change of tackle and adding another swivel link. The swivel link on the main line needs to be removed, and the line threaded through the swivel end of another one, then add a bead before the original swivel is tied back on the

← Feathers are one of the most common types of lure. They come in a wide range of colours and sizes.

main line. This now gives a form of sliding leger if the weight is clipped on to the swivel link that runs loose on the main line. A 2m trace of 20lb line is connected to the fixed swivel link with the lure on the end.

Changing to a single lure will still catch the odd mackerel, but the bigger lure will often gain the interest of a predatory bass. A bass will hit the lure with some force and pull the line off the reel as it uses the tide and the motion of the boat to try to swim to safety.

HOOKS

When it comes to buying a packet of hooks it should be the easiest thing in the world but beware, there is a staggering amount of different hook sizes, lengths and styles out there. Just to give an idea, you can buy semi-circle, circle, uptide, straight, offset, bait holder, spade end, eyed, barbed, barbless, fine wire, extra strong, stainless and bronzed – but let's keep it simple!

As a casual angler you need only to look at a very limited number of these. Firstly stick to sizes from 2 to 3/0. Don't buy stainless steel as they won't rot if hooks are lost in a fish. The Kamasan Aberdeen design (right) is good for most small fish in sizes 1 and 2, while the Sakuma range is good in sizes 1, 1/0 and bigger.

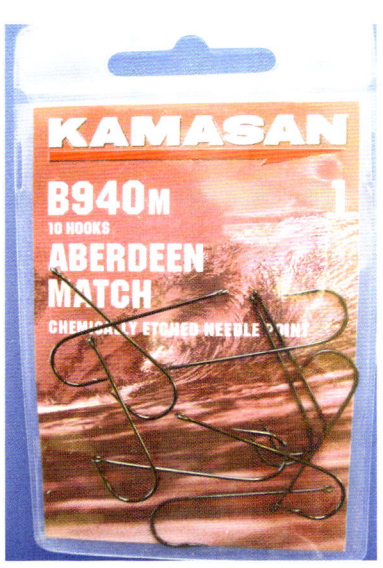

TOP TIP   Hooks range from size 32 (the smallest) to a 19/0 (a large, game-fish hook). Sizes 2 to 3/0 are mid-range hooks – suitable for the occasional angler.

BAIT

The wrapped black lugworm freeze best but even blow lug that go a bit soggy in the freezer will still catch plaice and dabs when thawed out. In the sea just about everything gets eaten so anything caught can be used as bait either live for the bigger species such as bass, cod and conger while small strips off any fresh fish caught will catch others. For example, any mackerel caught that are not wanted for the pot can be cut into strips and used in the same way as squid (see page 33). See pages 32–39 for more information on bait.

FROZEN BAIT

Keeping bait on a boat can be a problem, especially when going to sea for several days. If the boat has a small freezer, then a box of squid and a couple of packets of frozen lugworm will give you the chance to get fishing. Unwashed squid are a popular choice along with the well known Ammo blast frozen quality. Fresh lugworm wrapped in newspaper will stay in a usable condition for several days if kept in a fridge, or a couple of days somewhere cool. Ragworm will only last for one day if not kept in a fridge and are not suitable for freezing. When a shoal of mackerel is spotted, grab the rod with the feathers attached and try to catch a few. Any fish not eaten can be kept in the fridge or freezer, ready to use over a wreck or a reef for something bigger.

⬆ Frozen squid.

⬇ Unwashed squid is the popular choice for sea anglers.

LEAD HEADS

Drifting over wrecks can be a costly business, which is why lead heads have increased in popularity over the past decade. The design of the lead head puts the hook on the upper side of the weight so it's not the first bit to hit the bottom. The larger lead heads, weighing 6 to 8 ounces, complete with attractively coloured plastic tails, can be fixed directly to the main line swivel link. They should be lowered to the bottom then lifted and dropped so they bang on the seabed and over the wreck. The noise is enough to create interest from cod and pollack.

Many lead heads are made a lot smaller and should be fished on a one metre-long trace attached to a boom with a suitable weight. These are fished slightly differently as they are lowered to the bottom and then wound slowly up for 10 or 12 turns of the reel. The fish will chase the lure as it travels past them.

⬆ It is worth trying different colour combinations of lead heads to lure the fish.

GILLING

The term gilling comes from the method that first used artificial sand eels called Red Gills. Now there are several manufacturers making similar lures, but Red Gills still catch plenty of fish. The main difference from lead heads is that the lures are unweighted and fished on a long trace connected to a fixed boom. The boom is to keep the lure away from the main line as it is dropped to the bottom in deep water.

Gilling is one of the most exciting fishing methods. The lure is lowered to the bottom then slowly wound up as many as 35 turns off the bottom as the boat drifts over a wreck or reef. Pollack will follow the lure, and after plucking at it a few times, will eventually take it and crash-dive back towards the bottom. This first dive sets the heart racing until the fish is brought under control. The clutch needs to be set fairly lightly, otherwise a snap-off is inevitable.

The three artificial sand eels shown here are the Delta at the top, the original Red Gill and the Eddystone Eel. →

SHADS AND SIDEWINDERS

In recent years development of lures has seen the arrival of shads with paddle tails and the slimmer version called the sidewinder. Shads are an imitation fish and are adorned with the colours of many of the bait fish that cod and pollack feed on. Shads are worked on a shorter trace than the Red Gills and 'hop' along the bottom. The term 'cod hopping' came into being and this method has accounted for some enormous catches of prime cod. The slimmer sidewinders are a cross between the original sand eel lure and the shad, having a paddle tail that creates good movement in the water. These, too, have caught plenty of cod and have also become a particular favourite of bass fishermen.

Shads and sidewinders come in natural colours and can be amazingly lifelike. They come pre-hooked with super-sharp hooks. →

JELLYWORMS

The original plastic sand eels are still made, but anglers travelling to the USA found a range of soft plastic worms called jellyworms and eventually brought some back to the UK to try out. They proved to be sensational and were found to work in very little tide compared to the stiffer plastic ones that required a good tide run. They worked on the wrecks for the big pollack and the smaller ones picked up the inshore reef pollack. Probably the only drawback is that they are often ruined after catching a fish, as they bite through the soft plastic. They are best fished from a fixed boom with a 2m or 3m long trace and wound slowly up from the bottom. Slide the jellyworm up the shank of a size 2/0 or 4/0 hook with plenty of the body and tail hanging free to waggle and twist as it's retrieved.

LEAD WEIGHTS

You will be amazed at the different designs of lead weight available from the local tackle shop. Basically, the flatter ones are for fishing at anchor where the lead needs to stay in position on the seabed. Their low profile will pick up less of the tide and stay in one place better than, for example, a round one, which is used when the bait needs to be worked back with the tide until it gets back to the fish.

The more streamlined and torpedo-shaped leads are for fishing on the drift in deep water where they will drop quickly. There are watch-shaped and star-shaped ones, as well as weights with wire grips for fishing uptide. Each one will be made in weights from one or two ounces up to over one pound. Make sure you have a range of weights to cover all periods of the tide run.

← Lead weights come in an amazing choice of design, the flatter ones for holding the bottom and the more streamlined for getting down quickly.

BAITS

One thing that cannot be stated enough is the value of the bait for sea angling. In fact, the quality of the bait is the major factor in catches made by anglers whether at sea or on the shore. Luck only comes into it occasionally, while the use of the freshest and most correct bait for the species is the deciding factor for good catches 99% of the time. The best rod and reel in the world won't help at all unless you can tempt the fish on to your hook, and that's down to the bait. Fish have clearly defined preferences, and using the right one at the right time will definitely increase catches. Here are a few of the regularly used baits and which fish are likely to take them.

CUTTLEFISH FILLET AND STRIPS

Apart from the readily available mackerel and squid, cuttlefish makes good bait for bigger species as it is a firm meat that can't be ripped off by smaller fish. It can be used whole or in large fillets for big cod or conger, and when cut up into thin strips it will entice the larger black bream, bull huss and rays.

WHOLE CUTTLEFISH

To avoid small fish and to try for one of the bigger species, like conger eel or big cod, it pays to use a large, sturdy bait. Whole cuttlefish are ideal for this purpose as the flesh is very firm, and even if small fish nibble at some of the looser bits, there's always plenty left for the larger fish to find. They can be fished on a large single hook of 8/0 or even larger, but a two hook pennel rig (see pages 90–91) is more efficient as it holds the bait in a more natural shape.

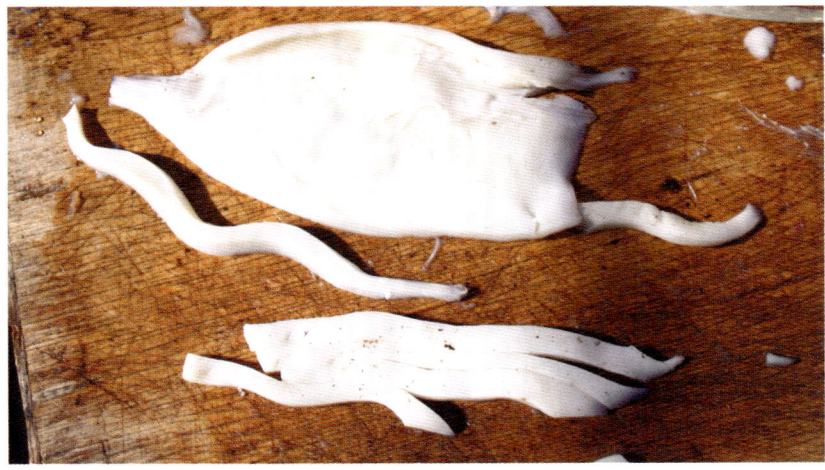

⬆ Cuttlefish cut into thin strips will entice the larger black bream, bull huss and rays.

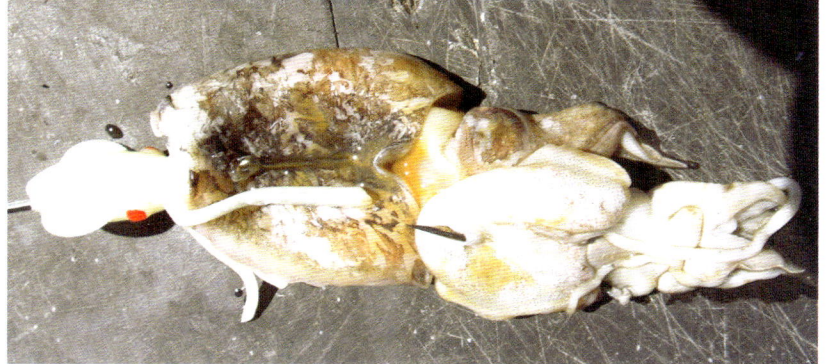

⬆ To entice bigger species like conger eel or large cod, use the cuttlefish whole.

CALAMARI SQUID

Calamari squid is available in 1lb or 5lb boxes and can be kept in the freezer for some time. It is good for many of the UK's resident species including cod, bull huss, bream, smooth hound, conger and rays. Squid stays on the hook well, and if a thin strip is hooked just once in one end it will flutter in the tide enticingly.

LUGWORM

Lugworm is one of the most widely used baits in the UK. Nearly all tackle shops keep them and they can be bought fresh or frozen, wrapped in newspaper.

The smaller blow lug are often available live and being small are sold by the pound rather than individually. Lugworm are popular bait because they catch such a wide range of sea fish. Codling, bream, whiting, plaice, pouting and dabs are the most likely species to be caught on lugworm. There are several others that will also be caught on occasions such as sole, gurnard and dogfish. It's an easy bait to use as it can be threaded up the shank of the hook to look very natural in the water. Lugworm give off a strong scent trail which makes them particularly good in dark waters.

Lugworm are extremely common around the British Isles and are, without doubt, the king of worm baits as they act as a great lure for fish. ➡

⬆ Ragworm are a superb sea fishing bait as they stay alive on the hook for a long time.

⬆ Frozen sand eels are a good standby bait and will catch several species.

RAGWORM

Ragworm are available in many tackle shops and are another bait that will catch plenty of species. They will attract all the same species as lugworm and a few more. Codling, whiting, bream, plaice, pouting and dabs are regularly caught on ragworm but they are also excellent for pollack, smooth hound and wrasse.

Ragworm don't need to be threaded up the shank of the hook. They work better if hooked once through the head. This allows them to swim naturally in the tide attracting the attention of any passing fish. They work well in clear water as the fish are attracted to their movement.

FROZEN SAND EELS

Flash frozen sand eels are convenient to keep and, used to fish at anchor, can catch a wide variety of fish. They pick up bass, rays, dogfish, plaice, brill, turbot and bull huss. They are a versatile bait as they work well on their own and when mixed with other baits such as squid and mackerel strip. Fished under a float they will pick up garfish.

Live sand eels make superb bait but are not easy to obtain. They work best on the drift for pollack and bass. It is possible to catch a supply on sand banks at slack tide using very small lures such as sabiki lures with size 6 hooks. These are sold in sets with four to six lures on a light trace, and if worked near the bottom with a shiny pirk as a weight, will pick up sand eels and their larger cousins the launce.

⬆ Hermit crabs are an under-valued bait which can attract a large number of species.

⬆ Fish love razors and you can find them littered on the beach following a storm.

HERMIT CRABS

Hermit crabs can be purchased at some tackle shops or they can be caught in a small crab pot dropped down from the side of the boat. Commercial fishermen get plenty in their crab and lobster pots and, with the right approach, may be persuaded to part with a few. Although hermit crabs are not a universal bait they will pick out certain species. They are a favourite food for smooth hounds and will generally out-fish any other offerings put down for them. Put them on whole for the big smooth hounds but break off the large claws for other fish. In the autumn and winter they will catch cod which spend much of their time feeding on brittle starfish, crabs and hermits.

LIVE RAZORS

After a severe gale or onshore storm the beaches can be littered with shellfish of all sorts. Most of them, such as slipper limpets, butterfish and mussels, will all catch fish in certain conditions, but the best ones to collect are the razorfish.

They are a conveniently-shaped bait, similar to a lugworm, that fish love and they will freeze successfully. They are another bait that can be purchased year-round from the local tackle shop. Bass, cod and flounders all love them and other fish such as dabs, whiting, pouting and plaice will take them especially when tipping off lugworm baits. Tipping off means adding a small piece of something different to a bait to increase the attraction.

← Lugworm can be collected by using a lugworm pump or bait pump as shown opposite or you can dig for lugworm using simply a spade or fork.

COLLECTING BAIT

There is so much more to sea angling than just dangling a line over the side and waiting for a bite. Anyone who appreciates this will want to know more about the way the tides influence fishing, why some fish only eat particular foods and how high up in the water they feed. The more knowledge gained, the more fish will be caught, as all this information eliminates a lot of wasted time trying things that do not work.

Having the best bait is usually the first thing anyone who fishes regularly realises is the key to success. Tackle shops can provide frozen bait, in many cases fresh worms, but collecting your own bait makes the whole fishing experience more satisfying. Rummaging around in rock pools looking for crabs and prawns can be rewarding, but one of the best methods is to collect your own lugworm using a bait pump.

Digging lugworm used to be a skilful business and hard work as well. The arrival of the bait pump from Australia a decade ago has changed all that. It's now possible to purchase a bait pump from your local tackle shop, wander down the beach at low tide and have a good chance of pumping up enough worms for a fishing session. There's still a certain technique to be mastered but it's something that can be accomplished fairly easily, and the thrill of providing your own bait adds greatly to the fishing experience.

PUMPING LUGWORM

First find a lugworm cast, push the pump down over it with one hand and draw up the handle with the other.

Lift the pump out and push out the contents – including the lugworm – on to the sand.

Collect the worm from the debris and store in a plastic bucket.

FREEZING SHELLFISH

More or less any shellfish will catch fish. The best method is to walk along the beach at low tide after an onshore gale. A variety of mussels, slipper limpets, butterfish, cockles and razorfish are all likely to have been blown in by the waves. To keep them for fishing it's best to blanch them. This involves pouring boiling water on them for a few seconds. It shouldn't be done long enough to cook them but it makes them stiffen up. They can now be removed from their shells easily and frozen. They will come out of the freezer firm and stay on the hook well. If they aren't blanched first, they unfreeze into a sloppy mess.

PREPARING SHELLFISH FOR FREEZING

First blanch the shellfish by pouring boiling water over them for a few seconds.

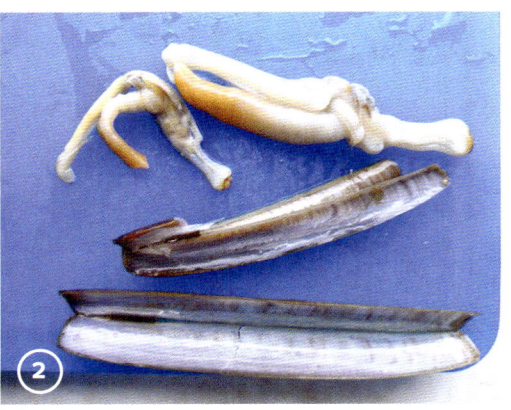

Remove the fish from their shells and freeze immediately.

← The coiled castings of the lugworm are a familiar sight on a beach at low tide. The animal itself is rarely seen except by those who use them as fishing bait.

KNOTS FOR FISHING

A step-by-step guide to tying knots

KNOTS

In this section we show the most popular knots used in boat angling around our coastline, using a step-by-step photographic guide (page 44 onwards). Knots are important, and many a good fish has been lost because of a badly tied knot. Sometimes this is because the knot has not been tightened enough or the wrong knot was used for the purpose.

BLOOD KNOT

We start off with the most simple of knots, the blood knot. This is used for all manner of things, such as connecting swivels to traces, hooks to snoods, lures to traces, but the knot needs to be pulled tight. Even so, American guides won't use it because it can slip under extreme pressure when fishing for harder fighting game fish such as tarpon. However, the blood knot works perfectly well for most of our fishing.

BLOOD LOOP OR DROPPER KNOT

The blood loop or dropper knot is a really good one to learn as it will put a stand-off loop in your trace line. This loop can be used to fix on a lure. Push the loop through the ring on the top of the lure, then pull the loop over the lure and pull tight. This knot is a little difficult to start with as it needs the knot held either side as the loop is pulled through. Try using your teeth to ease the line through.

UNI KNOT

The uni knot is another simple knot to tie but it's much more reliable than the blood knot. The knot is tightened up the line and then slid down to make a secure fixing. The uni knot is most unlikely to slip, which makes it a good one to perfect.

← Coloured line can be used as main line and leader line, but the body of traces and line to hooks should always be clear line.

LURE KNOT

The lure knot is formed up the line from the lure but it doesn't slip down. It's tightened a few centimetres from the eye of the lure to allow it to swim freely when pulled through the water. Like most knots it works best if it's moistened before finally being pulled tight.

STOP KNOT

An easy little knot used when float fishing to stop the float at the required depth. It is tied so that it holds firmly, but can be moved if required to change the depth of the float. It can also be used to stop bait flying up the line when casting.

LEADER KNOT

A leader knot is used for tying a thicker line to the thinner main line. Three or four metres of heavier line is used to take the shock out of casting when fishing uptide and can also help when controlling a fish at the side of the boat, as it gives something a bit more substantial to hold.

 **TOP TIP**
To prevent line burn, make sure you always moisten the line before pulling a knot tight.

BLOOD KNOT

The blood knot is a really basic knot that's widely used to tie line to swivels, lures and hooks. The knot must be pulled really tight, as it can slip under extreme pressure. Generally the blood knot is good enough for the fish we catch in the UK, but not for heavyweight fish such as conger and ray. All knots reduce line strength to some degree, and the blood knot can break as much as 10 per cent below the manufacturer's breaking strain. It can be made a little stronger by bringing the tag end through the loop next to the eye and then putting it back through the loop created. This is referred to as a tucked blood knot. Another tip is to put the line through the eye twice at the start of the knot as this adds a little more to the strength of the knot. Two lines of different thickness can be connected using two blood knots, although the knot can be a bit bulky.

HOW TO TIE A BLOOD KNOT

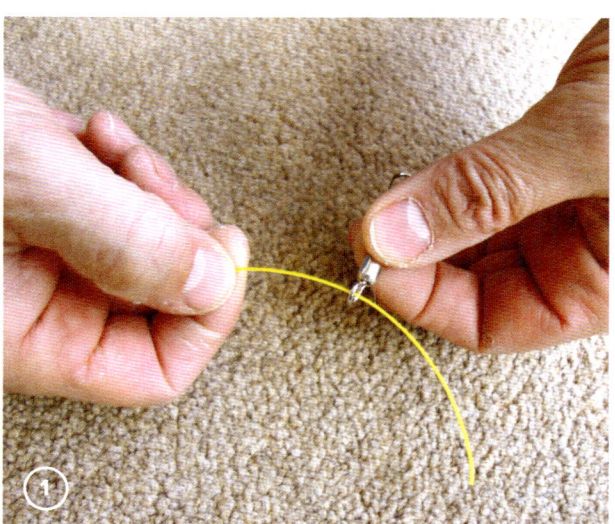

Push the line through the eye of the swivel.

TOP TIP The blood knot is a quick and easy knot but reduces line strength by around 10 per cent.

Then take five turns round the main line with the tag end.

Pass the tag end through the first loop next to the swivel.

Moisten the line then pull it tight and trim the end.

BLOOD LOOP OR DROPPER KNOT

The blood loop or dropper knot can be used to make a paternoster as it creates a loop or trace standing at right angles to the main trace. The loop can be threaded through the eye of a large hook or lure for fixing. For small hooks and lighter fishing, for example when fishing for bream, the loop can be cut close to the knot and the hook fixed on the single longer line. This creates a very neat trace that stands out from the main line.

The tightening of the dropper knot is a bit tricky as the loop needs to be pulled through while holding both ends of the main line in place. It's often easiest to hold the loop lightly with your teeth and gently pull it through whilst keeping hold of each end of the main line. The two knots should then be moistened before they are pulled together and finished with a firm steady pull.

HOW TO TIE A BLOOD LOOP

Form a large loop in the middle of a metre of line.

Wrap the end of the line round the loop six times.

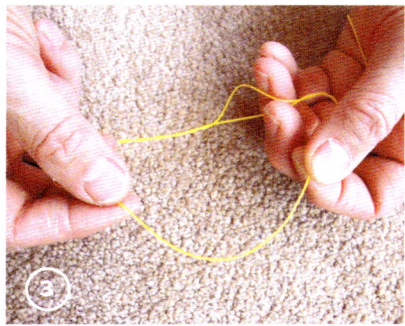

Push the large loop through the smaller loop that has formed between the sets of wraps.

Whilst holding each end with your hands, gently pull the loop through with your teeth.

Moisten the turns in the line and ease them tight.

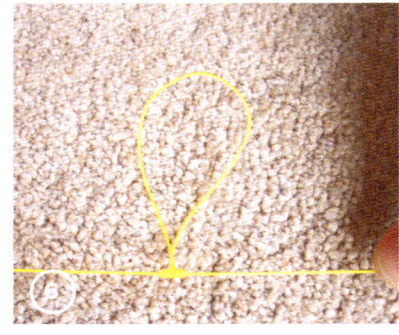

The finished blood loop can be threaded on to the eye of a large hook or lure for fixing.

For lighter fishing and small hooks cut the loop close to the knot.

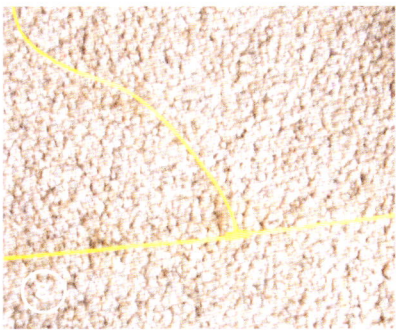

This leaves a double length of stand-off trace to tie on a hook.

UNI KNOT

The uni knot is more reliable than the blood knot as it's unlikely to slip under pressure. Once mastered it's just as easy as tying the blood knot. Because the uni knot maintains a high percentage of its breaking strain it is widely used by game fishermen who don't trust the blood knot for hard fighting fish.

Many knots can lose as much as 20 per cent of the line strength but the uni maintains over 90 per cent. For example, a 20lb line with a bad knot could break at around 16lb, whereas a uni knot would ensure it would break at over 18lb. This could be crucial if a really big fish is hooked. Make sure the knot is moistened with saliva before it's finally tightened.

The uni knot is versatile and can be adapted for many purposes, including connecting hooks, swivels and lures with a loop, and joining two lines together.

HOW TO TIE A UNI KNOT

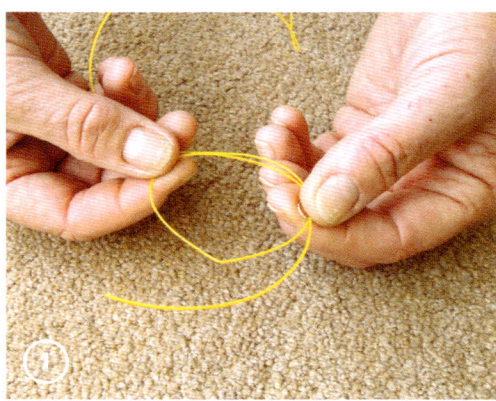

Thread about 30cm of line through the eye of the hook or swivel. Bring the line back round to form a loop and hold with thumb and forefinger against the eye.

Tuck the end of the line through the loop and wrap the end round the two lines at least four times.

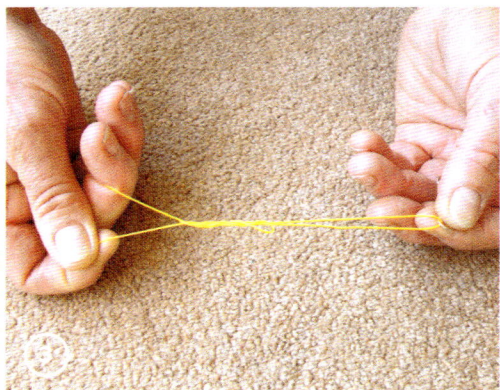

Pull the knot tight while still a little way up the main line.

Moisten and slide the knot down to the eye, tighten again and trim the tag end.

TOP TIP Don't be put off if you don't get this knot or the blood loop first time – they take a little practice.

LURE KNOT

To get the best out of a trolling lure it's important to use the right knot. It has been found that tightening a blood knot tight to the lure can result in the lure tipping over or not running naturally. To get over this problem a knot that doesn't tighten on to the eye of the lure was tried and found to make all the difference. The lure knot can be tightened a little way up from the lure giving it a much more natural movement in the water.

Tie a loose overhand knot in the line before the end is pushed through the eye of the lure, otherwise it can be difficult to do afterwards, especially if the lure has two sets of treble hooks on it. Like most knots formed in nylon, moistening it with a little saliva will help pull the knot in more tightly.

It is important to trail the lure close to the boat to start with to make sure it's running properly. If it's spinning or lying over on its side you may need to retie the knot.

HOW TO TIE A LURE KNOT

Tie an overhand knot in the trace line and leave it loose. Push the end of the line through the lure. Then take the end of the line through the overhand knot.

Wrap the line round the trace above the overhand knot three times.

Bring the end back and push it through the loop that's formed.

Moisten, pull tight, and trim off the tag end. The knot won't slip down and it allows the lure to move freely.

THE STOP KNOT

This knot will stop the float from sliding up the line but can be moved so that the depth can be changed.

Cut a short length of line, form a loop and hold it alongside the main line. Put the end through the loop and round both lines four times.

Moisten the knot and pull it tight.

Trim the ends and you have your stop knot.

THE LEADER KNOT

A leader is a line of heavier breaking strain that's added to the main line to take the shock of casting. It is also a great help when controlling an active fish at the side of the boat ready for the landing net. Thirdly, while fishing over rough ground or wreckage it will take knocks better. The leader needs to be at least twice the length of the rod so that there are a few winds on the reel when casting.

Form an overhand knot in the thicker line and push the end of the thinner line through the loop. Then pull the knot very tight to hold the thinner line.

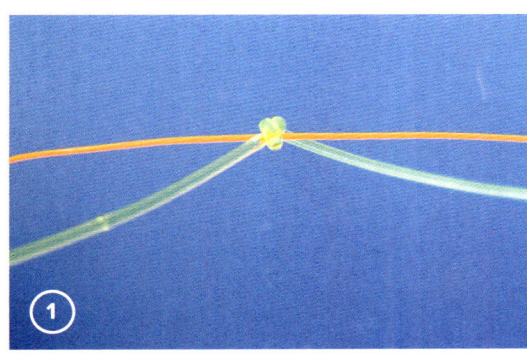

Twist the thinner line six times around the thicker line and bring the tag end back through the loop next to the knot.

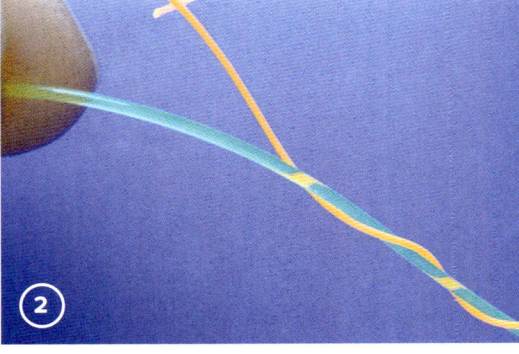

Moisten and slide the knot up tight and trim the ends.

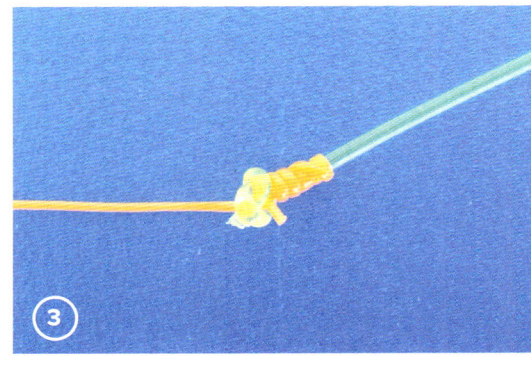

TROLLING
Fishing on the move

TROLLING

One of the least demanding ways of catching fish is trolling, or pulling a lure along behind the boat as you motor along at a steady 5 to 7 knots. At the correct speed and using the correct tackle, trolling produces a motion that mimics a live fish ready to be eaten by a bigger predator. The fish you catch using this method will be predatory fish that swim in mid-water chasing the shoals of whitebait and sprats. Your lures flashing through the water will put them in the attack mode.

A set of feathers can be pulled along behind the boat for mackerel, and an old fashioned mackerel spinner is still widely used in Cornwall to good effect. This is all well and good if mackerel are your only target, but if you fancy a nice plate of sea bass for your meal you need to change over to a proper trolling lure. This will mean using a Rapala, Red Gill, sidewinder or Eddystone type of artificial lure. The rig for using this type of lure is shown opposite. All that needs to be added is a 2m to 3m trace of 20lb nylon, then tie on the chosen lure. The lure needs to run below the surface. If it can be seen coming out of the water either reduce the speed of the boat or increase the weight.

⬇ Predatory fish such as bass and pollack will see the lure as an injured fish and strike from below.

RIGGING UP

This simple rig for trolling uses a free sliding swivel link on the main line for the weight. It allows the weight to be changed easily to get the lure to the right depth without having to undo anything else.

SIMPLE RIG FOR TROLLING

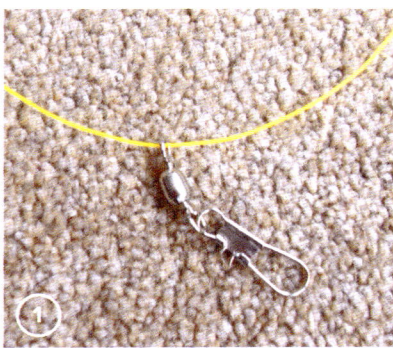

Thread a line through the swivel link.

Then add a bead.

Tie on another swivel link.

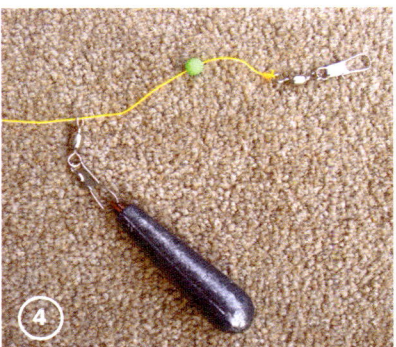

Clip on a lead and it is ready to tie on a trace to the lure.

EASY PICKINGS

Artificial lures are all designed to perform differently in the water. Some waggle side to side in a very enticing way while others dive up and down or skittle around in an erratic fashion. They are all designed to make the predatory fish think something is up, and they present an easy target. A fit fish with no injuries is not easy to catch, which is why bass and pollack are always on the lookout for anything that might not tax them too much. To chase a fish or a lure expends vital energy which all fish and animals have to conserve as much as possible. If they tire themselves out and show signs of weakness, there's always something much bigger and hungrier that will hunt them down, such as dolphins and seals.

The Rapala lures are fitted with two or even three treble hooks. This is because the fish sometimes attack from the side, and the second hook makes sure of connecting with them. The lures are fitted with a vane at the front which makes them dive below the surface. The sharper the angle of the vane the deeper the lure works. It's always worth having two or three lures with different settings, as sometimes the fish may be feeding deeper and a change of lure could find them.

← The vane attached to the front of the lure will produce a wobbly swimming motion when the lure is pulled through the water.

LURES FOR TROLLING

BASS ASSASSIN

These lures are a tried and tested bass catcher. They can be trolled behind a boat or used for gilling over a wreck. They are a combination of a lead head, a muppet and an artificial eel and are manufactured by Trace Ace Tackle.

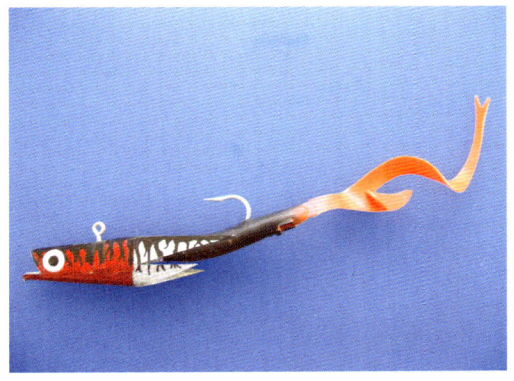

MACKEREL DIVER

This lure has a solid body painted to represent a mackerel, and it gains its movement from the vane on the nose that sends the lure diving and dipping as it's pulled along behind the boat.

JOINTED PLUG

The body of this lure is made in two parts giving it more movement than the one above. It will still dive and dip but it also creates a waggling motion with the separate tail section.

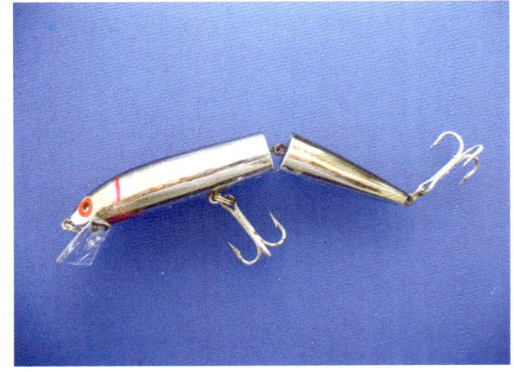

OTHER LURES

The lures shown here can be used for trolling and are useful at other times as well.

DEXTER WEDGE

The Dexter wedge can be used for casting to bass, or can be fixed below a set of feathers. For casting it can be clipped directly to the swivel on the end of the main line. Cast the lure away from the boat, allow a few seconds for it to sink then work it back towards the boat with a series of jerks. This makes the lure flip up in the tide then flutter down, attracting predatory fish. When used with the feathers it can catch species such as bass, cod and pollack as well as the expected mackerel.

THE POPPER PLUG

The popper plug can also be cast away from the boat and worked back. The difference is that it floats on the surface and each jerk of the rod makes a distinct popping sound as the concave nose is pulled into the waves. Bass in particular will be attracted to the popping sound and can sometimes be seen following the lure just before they strike. This plug works best if cast over or near weed beds where the bass will be lurking.

EDDYSTONE PLUG

This plug is a combination lure with a solid body and the tail of an artificial eel. It's an excellent mix as it has the bulk of a fish and the attraction of a soft tail that is designed to wobble enticingly.

MUPPETS

These muppet lures will come into their own when travelling down south towards Gibraltar. Troll them behind the boat and you could bring dorado and the smaller tuna such as the skipjack and the bonito to the boat. Both are excellent on a barbecue.

WHAT'S THAT FISH?

MACKEREL

The fish that are most readily caught trolling will be mackerel, especially if you are using feathers or a string of silvery lures. Mackerel are an excellent food provided they are eaten fresh, and catching your own means they couldn't be fresher. They are also a great bait as nearly every other fish in the sea will eat mackerel. Mackerel are very much a shoal fish, and if one is caught, usually several others will be found in the same area.

As soon as a fish is safely in the boat give it a sharp tap on the head with something heavy to stop it jumping about and making a mess. Once fish are located it's worth circling around to relocate the shoal.

⬆ Catching mackerel on trolled lures is great fun. If you fancy one for dinner they are great to eat.

← A garfish is edible but a bit off-putting when cooked as the bones go green, but apart from this the flesh is quite pleasant.

GARFISH

Another fish you may catch while trolling with feathers is the strange looking garfish, sporting a long, pointed beak. A garfish fights quite differently from a mackerel as it likes to leap out of the water like its cousins of the billfish family; the marlin and sailfish.

The long nose is not dangerous, but due care should be taken when handling a garfish as they are a lively eel-like shape. If they are not required for eating, put them back as gently as possible; they are all part of the food chain.

HORSE MACKEREL

The scad, better known as a horse mackerel, is another fish that is regularly caught trolling with feathers. It's a much more bony fish than the mackerel and for this reason not often eaten. They are used as live bait by professional bass fishermen, as they make particularly good bait, being much more hardy than mackerel.

↑ Scad, or horse mackerel, can be found throughout UK waters during early summer and autumn.

↑ The bass can be lured with any number of baits, so the choice is up to you.

BASS

Change the lure to an imitation sand eel, silver spinner, sidewinder lure or storm shad, and it could be taken by the highly prized bass or a reef pollack. When in a feeding frenzy the bass will attack almost any trolled lure. Bass are one of the most sought-after species for sea anglers. Many anglers specialise in targeting bass as they can be caught on a wide variety of baits, fight like the devil and make good eating.

CHECK YOUR CHARTS

Bass are most likely to be picked up if you troll close to a shoal of fish on the surface, as they will be feeding below. They also lurk around reefs and wrecks, so it's worth steering close to any obstruction you see on the chart or GPS, provided you have plenty of water under you. While trolling near rocky headlands and inshore reefs there's also a good chance of picking up a pollack.

SECURE THE ROD

Once the line has been let out far enough and the lure is working just below the surface, the rod should be set up in a rod holder or propped against the gunwale. If the boat doesn't have rod holders fitted, the rod should be secured with a rope or some sort of makeshift clip to prevent it being pulled over the side.

The clutch should be loosened so that line can be pulled off the reel if a large fish is hooked. The rod may be held if someone else is at the helm but it can be a waiting game, and the better option is to set up the rod and keep an eye out for any action. The first indication of a fish is usually when the rod bends over and the line peels off as the fish runs.

One sure way to know there's a fish on the line is to leave the ratchet on. This way, when the fish steams off with the lure it will be accompanied by a loud noise. Now's the time to grab hold of the rod and be ready to strike into the fish. Everyone on board will be longing for you to click off the ratchet as soon as possible as it can get on their nerves very quickly. One last reminder: don't forget to set your clutch so that line can be peeled off the reel, otherwise the rod will be pulled over the back of the boat if something decent grabs the lure.

TOP TIP Gulls are a good indication of surface activity, improving your chance of hooking a bass.

FISH IDENTIFIER

DRIFTING
Fishing on the drift

DRIFTING

The biggest advantage of fishing on the drift is the amount of ground that is covered. It's a great way to locate the fish, and once found they can be targeted by going over the same area several times. Modern GPS units show exactly where the boat has travelled, so it's easy to go back and do the same drift again. The biggest snag is that more tackle is lost drifting as hooks catch rocks, weed and other obstructions as easily as they hook fish.

Using a paternoster rig that's two hooks above the weight, losses can be kept to a minimum by allowing the lead to just touch bottom and then winding up half a turn on the reel.

Keep letting the weight touch the bottom now and again. If the area is particularly rocky get someone to keep an eye on the echo sounder so that they can warn everyone if there's a sudden change of depth.

↓ The well-equipped *Sea Mistress* drifting off Weymouth.

RIGGING UP

To get set up for bottom fishing on the drift you need to take off the swivel link on the end of the main line, thread on the plastic boom and reconnect the link. Use a trace around four feet in length and made of 20lb line. Fix a size one hook at the end of the trace, and to double your chances another one halfway along the boom. A couple of bright coloured beads threaded on the line above the hooks will increase your chance of catching. For flatfish you may need to purchase some lugworm or ragworm as these are the preferred baits. Putting a bead between the boom and the swivel stops the swivel jamming in the end of the boom. The trace length can be varied to suit the conditions, the rule being the stronger the tide, the longer the trace. If a long trace is put down when the tide is slack, a tangle is nearly always the result.

HOW TO RIG A TUBI BOOM

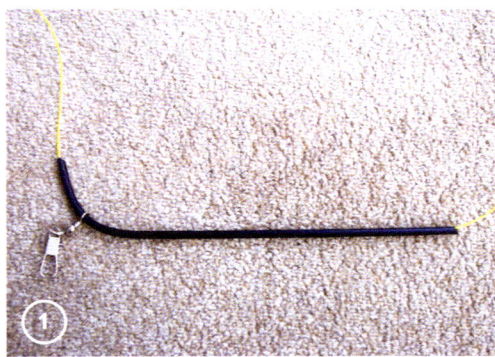

Thread the main line through the boom.

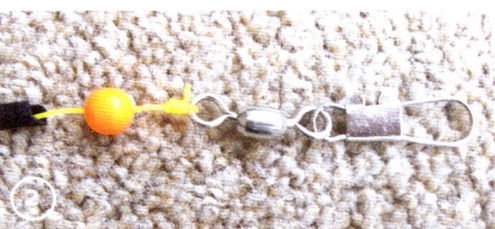

Slide on a bead and tie on a swivel link.

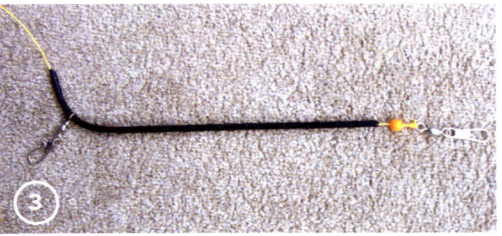

Put on a lead and it is ready for the trace.

LURES

One excellent way of catching all sorts of species is to drift the boat across a mixture of sand and rough ground. For many of the species, the mini shrimp and hokkai lures are ideal, and tipping the hook with a thin strip of squid or mackerel will catch many species such as bream, codling, whiting, pouting and gurnard.

Another productive way to fish on the drift is with a paternoster rig. This means having two hooks above the lead and these can be tied on using the blood loop (see pages 46–47). Tie one hook about 30cm from the bottom and a second one at about 60cm up. Keep the line from the main rig to the hook fairly short at around 25cm so they won't tangle. Squid is readily available in 1lb boxes from tackle shops and fishmongers and will keep for a long time in the freezer.

If your fancy is for a nice plaice or dab, the end tackle needs to be changed to what is called a leger rig using a plastic boom. These booms are very cheap but are needed to keep the trace away from the main line as you drop the tackle down to the seabed.

A quick and cheap way to rig up is the same as for lure fishing, using two swivel links, but shortening the trace to one metre in length.

⬆ A set of mini shrimps can catch many different varieties of fish.

BITES

Drifting with the mini shrimps will produce strong bites with the fish often hooking themselves. Some fish swim up from below the lures and lift the lead, giving the rod a light feeling as if the weight has come off. Lift the rod up steadily and you'll feel the fish. Pollack are one species that often take in this way.

With the legered rig dragging the weight along the bottom, it sometimes pays to let off one or two metres of line once a bite is felt before winding in This allows the slower feeding fish to get a good hold on the bait.

The one drawback to fishing on the bottom while drifting is the chance of snagging on rocks or other obstructions. The faster the drift, the more tackle will be lost. Sometimes the hook will straighten and allow the rig to come free, but tackle will usually be lost so it's a good idea to have a few spare traces made up and ready to clip on in case this happens.

⬆ Use your finger to detect bites.

BAIT

PREPARING SQUID

One of the easiest and most durable baits is squid. It can be kept in a fridge for long periods and stays on the hook well. Cut the squid into narrow strips and hook just once in one end so it flutters about in the tide. Most fish will take it down in one gulp but if several bites are missed and the bait is stolen, threading the bait up the hook shank could increase the catch rate. The head of a squid is a particularly good bait for large bream, and dogfish like them as well. Using a whole squid will catch all the bigger species such as ray, conger, bull huss and tope, while most other species will take strips of the flesh.

Other baits such as lugworm and ragworm are excellent but are not always available, especially if you are cruising to strange places or anchoring in a secluded bay with no town within reach. This is why a few packets of squid kept in a small freezer will mean there's always bait available. A few frozen lugworm will provide another option if sourced when available.

PREPARING SQUID FOR BAIT

⬆ Peel off the outer skin and wings to leave the pure white flesh. If the flesh looks pink, then it has been refrozen.

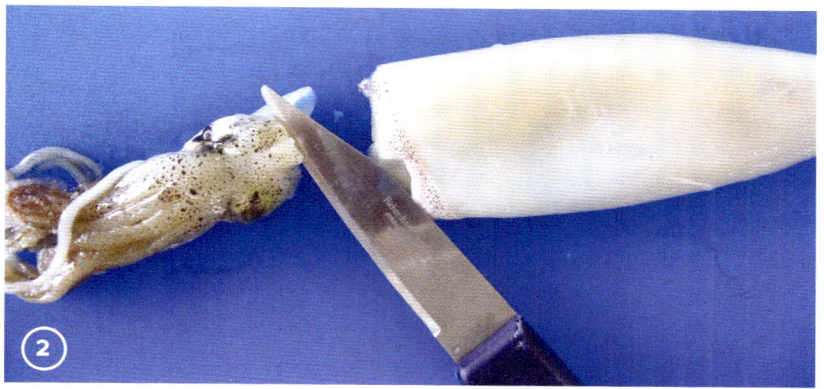

↑ Cut off the head. Keep it for bait as half a head is serious bream bait.

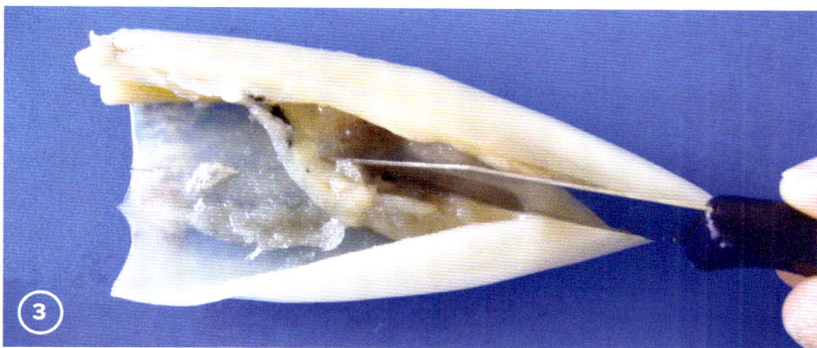

↑ Slice open the body of the squid. Remove the contents.

↑ Cut the flesh into long, narrow strips. These finished strips can be hooked on to either hokkai lures or mini shrimps.

FLATFISH

One species that is caught more than most while drifting is plaice. A trace of around 1.5m with several beads and maybe a flasher above the bait is the tackle to use. Baits vary from area to area but generally they are a mixture of worm fish and shellfish.

One excellent bait is a lugworm pushed up the shank of the hook, then hook a ragworm through the head and leave it hanging so it can wriggle naturally. Finally a long thin strip of squid is hooked once in the end. This looks great in the tide and catches a lot of good plaice each year.

Lugworm or ragworm can be used on their own or with a razorfish if available. If you feel a bite while drifting for plaice allow a couple of metres of line off the spool so the fish has time to get the bait down. Often this isn't necessary because the fish grabs the bait in one go and stays on the bottom. The boat drifts on and the line tightens into the fish and it's hooked.

As plaice spawn early in the year they are not at their best in the spring when they move back inshore. Summer fish are much fatter as they begin to roe up again. As autumn arrives they move off once again

← This spring plaice will have recently spawned.

while in prime condition. Plaice love to feed over mussel beds that are covered in the tiny yellow and black pea mussels. This is why black and yellow beads seem to work better than others on plaice traces.

Plaice are widely distributed, found anywhere between Norway and the Mediterranean, and they take five to six years to reach maturity at around 40cm. All of these three rigs are proven plaice catchers, yet they are all slightly different. The top one uses black and yellow beads with a f asher or spoon to attract attention. The middle one has just beads including a luminous one. The bottom rig is a combination of pearl beads, a flasher and a luminous bead in the middle. Whether these beads and flashers make a difference is often debated, but as most anglers who have regular success with plaice use rigs similar to this it probably speaks for itself. Hook size can be from size 1 to 2/0 depending on the bait being used and the size of the fish expected.

⬇ Three rigs that catch plaice, all with some beads or an attractor.

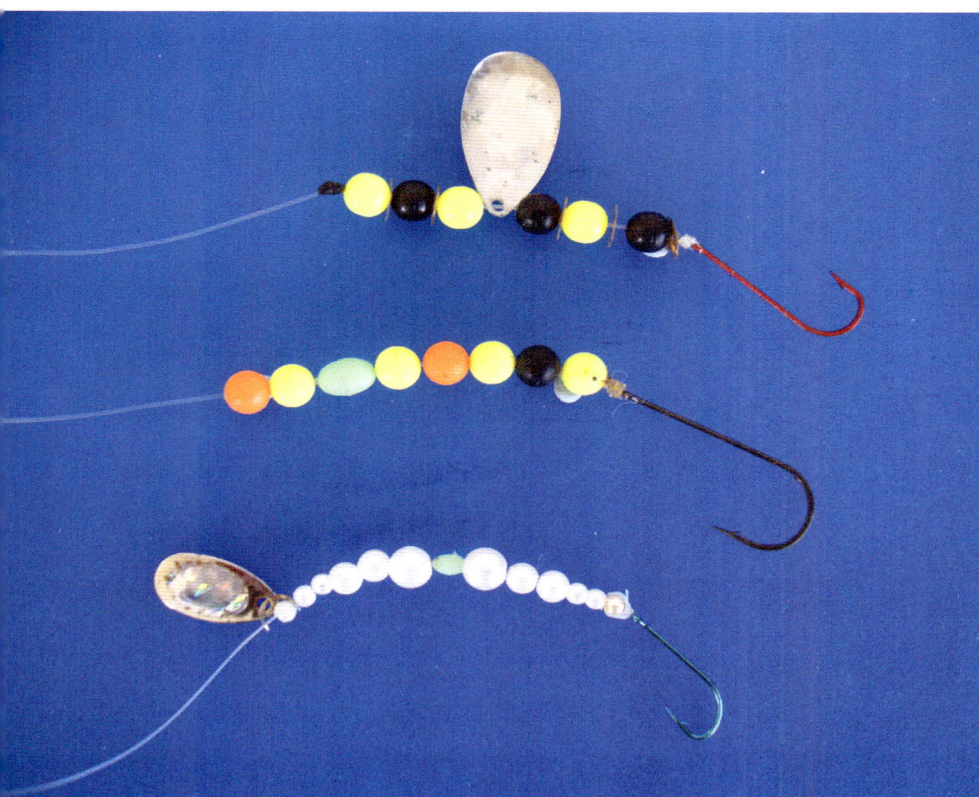

WHAT'S THAT FISH?

BASS

Bass is a striking looking fish with large, silvery scales and sharp erect dorsal fins when fresh out of the sea. It can be caught using all the methods mentioned in this book – trolling, drifting or anchored – and gives powerful runs and head thumping when hooked. It will fight all the way to the boat, not giving up until the end. It is also a very sought-after food source and has been subjected to heavy commercial pressure in recent years. It is found in all European waters and down to the Mediterranean Sea.

⬆ This bass was caught using a whole mackerel as bait.

POUTING

The pouting is a small but deep-bodied fish with a bronze back and white belly. It can have broad stripes if caught near reefs or wrecks. These fish are just about everywhere, but they tend to congregate around any obstruction such as inshore reefs and wrecks. They are edible, but not the most favoured of fish as they are a bit bony and they go off quickly if left in the sun. Their stomach juice is so powerful it can eat its way out in a matter of hours.

⬆ Pouting can be a nuisance as they can form large shoals and will grab any bait put down for the intended species.

BLACK BREAM

The most prolific bream in UK waters is the black bream. It is a striking looking fish, fights well on light tackle and it is in the same family as the bass, so it tastes good. When fishing in the West Country and down the coast of France and Portugal, other bream such as the red bream, pandora and couches bream add variety to the catches. Be careful when handling bream as the dorsal fins are very sharp.

Black bream give good sport on light tackle and can strip the bait in seconds. It can be quite a knack to catch them and it may mean using hooks as small as size 6 before you can hook them on a regular basis. They arrive off the south coast of England in big shoals as early as April and stay until the autumn.

GURNARD

There are three different sorts of gurnard most frequently caught around the UK coastline. The red gurnard is bright red with yellow under the gill cover. The biggest of the gurnards is the tub gurnard, which is a duller red but has a large pectoral fin with a distinct blue edge. The grey gurnard is the smallest of the three, and is generally caught in deeper water. As its name suggests, it is a dull grey when caught.

Although the body of the gurnard is hard and scaly, when skinned it makes a very pleasant meal and is a very underrated fish.

↑ The black bream can be found close to British shores between the summer month of June and September.

↑ The tub gurnard with its distinctive blue edging around the pectoral fin.

⬆ The grey gurnard, the smallest of the three.

⬆ The red gurnard is a bottom feeding fish; it uses its leg-like pectoral fins to search the seabed for its food.

FISH IDENTIFIER

⬆ Cod are not so prolific in UK waters.

COD

A favourite fish for most boat anglers is the cod, but in recent years the catches have drooped off badly. Mainly caught in winter, they are still found in summer on offshore reefs and wrecks. It has a deep body with a green and brown spotted back and a single barbel under its chin. They can be caught on lures such as sidewinders, lead heads and soft plastics, and baits including lugworm, squid, cuttlefish and crab.

SMOOTH HOUND

The smooth hound is a small crab-eating shark that will often take a squid bait. It looks like a cross between a dogfish and a tope, but can be identified by its flat, grating teeth rather than sharp, pointed ones.

The flesh is pleasant to eat apart from the females in pup, as they have a strong taste of ammonia. A smooth hound will give a good account of itself when hooked, and if one in double figures takes the bait, it will take some skill to boat it successfully.

⬆ The smooth hound is a member of the shark family with a pointed head and oval eyes.

WRASSE

Drifting across rough ground, there is every chance of catching a ballan wrasse, particularly if using ragworm for bait. The ballan wrasse is a deep-bodied fish with a fairly small mouth, thick rubbery lips and is armed with teeth.

They come in a wide range of colours. They are mostly a dull green or brown, but they can be bright red or orange. They aren't very good eating as they are a bit bony, so put them back carefully. Don't be disappointed if they just turn belly-up and float away on the tide as they are not the hardiest of sea fish.

⬅ Wrasse take bait with an enthusiasm which makes them very exciting to catch.

FISHING AT ANCHOR

Bottom fishing

FISHING AT ANCHOR

Fishing at anchor requires a different approach to fishing on the drift or trolling. It opens up the chance of several other bottom feeding species and is a nice leisurely way to fish after a long day's cruise or during a stopover. This is when the shorter rod and a multiplier reel will be the better option, as it can deal with weights of up to a pound that may be required to get the bait firmly on the seabed. There is also a chance of a bigger fish such as a bull huss, conger eel or ray.

Fishing on the bottom can be a waiting game, the more so for bigger fish as the scent of the bait will draw them towards it. Smaller fish will sometimes bite as soon as the bait touches the bottom as they have to compete with other small fish. With a running leger setup, use a one or two hook flowing trace of 1.5m. Bait could be a mackerel or squid strip on the bottom hook and maybe a worm on the other one.

First bites can be just a short rattle on the rod tip. Don't pick the rod up yet but allow the bite to develop. If the fish hooks itself it will make it obvious it's time to wind in, as the rod will bend and keep nodding.

One good idea is to have a couple of running booms set up in case you snag the bottom and lose one. Use about half a metre of 30lb line threaded through the boom. Put a small swivel on the top and a bead and swivel at the bottom. These can be clipped on to the swivel link on the main line easily without a lot of fiddling about. With some spare traces in a rig wallet changes can be made easily and effectively. Clip on another weight and you will be fishing again in no time.

 **TOP TIP** There's always a chance of hooking one of the larger species while fishing at anchor.

ONE UP ONE DOWN RIG

This is a good first option rig when trying a new venue. It will catch free-swimming fish off the bottom and present a separate bait for the bottom feeders. Clear nylon is recommended for traces; colour lines are used here for the sake of clarity.

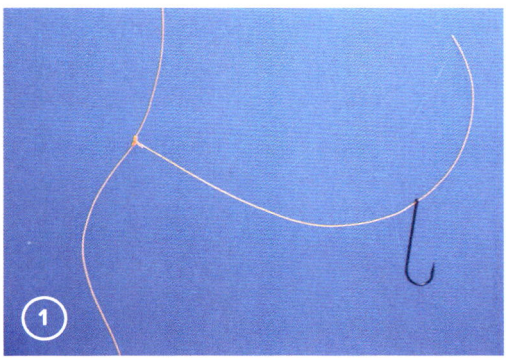

Tie a dropper knot (see pages 46–47) in a metre-long length of 25lb trace line. Cut the loop and tie on a size 1 hook. This one will be baited with a strip of squid or a ragworm.

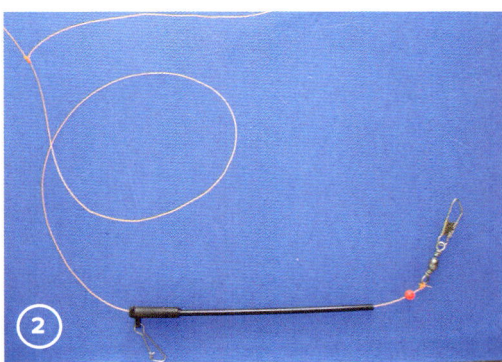

Thread on a running boom and set it half a metre below the hook already in place. Put on a bead and a swivel link to maintain the half metre.

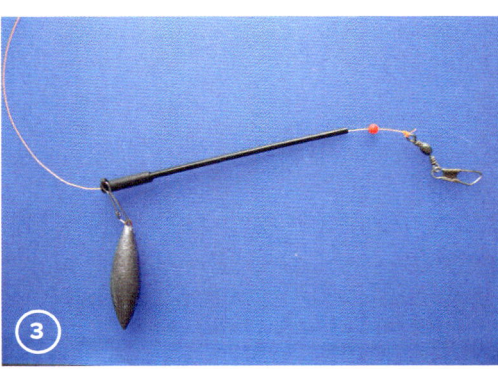

Put on a trace about 60cm in length with a hook slightly larger such as a 2/0 and bait with mackerel strip. Now you're ready to go.

GROUND BAIT

When fishing at anchor there's no doubt that getting some sort of scent trail going entices the fish to work up tide in search of the food source. Shark anglers can confirm this statement, although they do it mainly on the drift. Introducing a flow of mashed up fish, squid, worm or crab in the area of your bait will definitely improve catches. This is particularly noticeable with black bream, whiting, dogfish, rays, smooth hound, spur dogfish, tope and even flatfish. To clarify, ground baiting is also known in some parts as chumming or rubby-dubby.

PREPARATION

The problem is getting the ground bait to where you want it. Because of the depth of water and the tide it is not easy to accomplish. It's time consuming if you are trying to fish as well. But the advantages it creates make it well worthwhile. One way to make life easier is preparation. Getting a bucket of fish scraps, worm, squid and crab, all cut up and crushed, with a little pilchard oil mixed in, will save so much time when you get on the fishing grounds. But this is not always possible, as you may have to rely on catching some fresh mackerel you can mash up as the ground bait. Don't forget to have something suitable for reducing the fish down to a paste such as a chunky bit of wood and a sturdy bucket.

WHAT'S NOT EFFECTIVE

There are a few ways to use ground bait from an anchored boat and one of the least effective, but the easiest to do, is to keep all the bits of bait and leftover fish from previous trips and freeze them down in a mesh bag. This can then be tied to the anchor and left to thaw out, over a period of time. The reason this is not perfect is the distance it puts the scent away from the baits. With 100 yards of anchor rope out and the lines streaming up to 40 or 50 yards behind the boat it creates a big gap between bait and scent trail. Any slight breeze can move the boat well off the line of the scent trail. All this does is to take the fish away from you.

OVER THE STERN

Instead of tying the bag of frozen chum to the anchor, it can be lowered over the stern attached to a large weight. This puts the scent in the right place but can be a real pain, as the fishing lines can easily get caught up in the line of the bag or the bag itself. A much better method, and a lot easier to do is the supermarket plastic bag trick. All you need is a plastic bag, a 1lb weight fixed to your main line, with end tackle removed. Turn the plastic bag inside out and tie the lead to the bottom of the bag. Now put the bag back the right way and fill with your ground bait or rubby-dubby. Loosely twist the top of the bag round the main line and lower over the side and drop to the bottom.

When it hits the seabed, jerk it up and down to turn the bag inside out and let the contents out and then wind back up. This is best done with a spare rod so you can carry on fishing.

THE EDGE

Many weird and wonderful bait droppers have been created to do this job, with a box that opens on impact when it hits the bottom. One ready-made stainless steel ground bait box that works very well is called 'The Edge'. The box is filled with the ground bait, then carefully closed and lowered on a sturdy cord over the side. When the box hits the bottom, it opens up and allows the scraps of fish bits out and puts the scent trail right where your baits are. It does take time and effort but like most things in life the more effort you put in, the more you get out.

There are a couple of things to watch out for using the Edge. As both sides fly open when the lead hits the bottom, it can do the same thing in the boat if the lead hits the gunnel or anything else in the boat. This can result in some messy ground bait all over yourself or the deck. When filling the Edge lay it down on one side on a cutting board or somewhere that doesn't matter getting a bit messy getting a bit of mess on. Lift the top side and fill with your fishy offering and close the lid. Lift carefully, holding both sides in place before hanging it over the side and dropping to the bottom attached to some sturdy cord.

Place the Edge on one side and fill with your rubby-dubby.

Carefully lower over the side and drop it to the bottom.

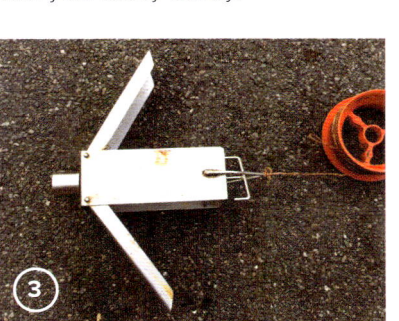

Lift and drop it a couple of times to make sure both sides fly open, releasing all the ground bait.

BOTTOM FISHING

KEEP CONTROL

Lower the tackle down steadily, under control, so it doesn't tangle on the way down. Then after it hits the seabed lift it gently a couple of times, feeding out line until it hits the bottom again. The tide will take the weight downtide a little before it settles.

As the tide increases or decreases during the fishing session, so the weights will need to be adjusted to allow the rig to stay firmly on the bottom. At slack tide the weight can be cut to as little as a couple of ounces. The rod can be held all the time and bites felt through the rod, or it can be propped up on the gunwale and bites will be registered by movements on the rod tip. It's advisable to set the clutch, so that line will pull off the reel if a big fish takes the bait, as many a rod has been pulled over the side when left unattended.

With experience, the bites can be recognised, as each fish has its own way of picking up the bait.

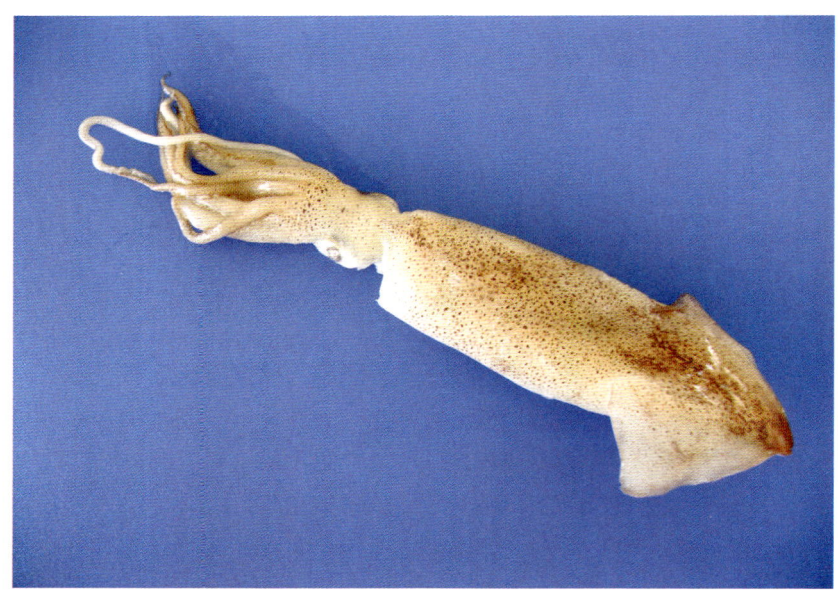

⬆ Using large bait like this whole squid can attract some seriously large fish.

USEFUL EQUIPMENT

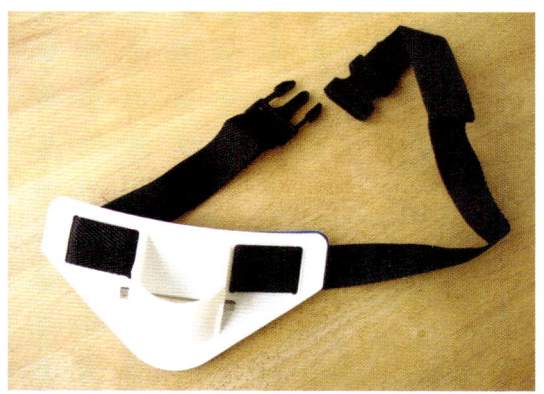

BUTT PAD
If you do find yourself fishing for congers, either in your own boat or a charter boat, you may find a butt pad very helpful in protecting your stomach and groin area.

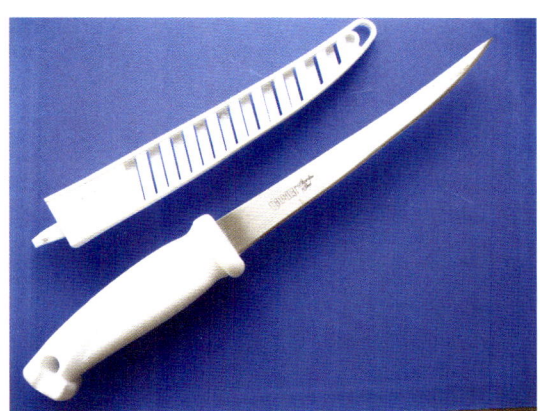

KNIFE
Every boat angler should have a sharp knife somewhere close at hand, not only to cut up bait or fillet but also as a safety measure. When emergencies occur, such as a rope round the propeller, the knife needs to be somewhere handy so that swift action can be taken to cut the rope.

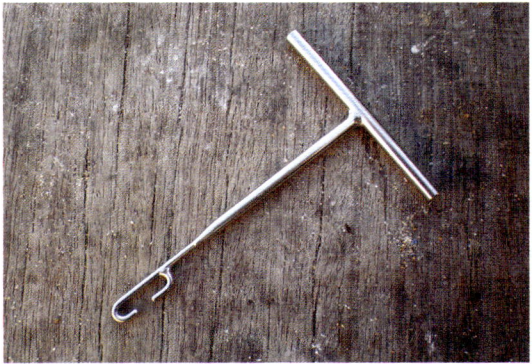

T-BAR
The T-bar makes unhooking large fish at the side of the boat much easier than getting them onboard where they can cause damage and a mess.

BAIT PRESENTATION

Why do I need a pennel rig? The reason is that it's not easy to put on large bait without it balling up round the shank of the hook. Elasticated cotton can do the trick in some cases, but for large squid and cuttlefish bait for instance, the pennel rig is the answer. Many anglers like to put on several squid when they go cod fishing in the winter. The bait can be threaded on the bottom hook and then the top hook is fixed in position by turning the trace line round the hook shank. The hook is then pushed through the tail end of the squid holding it in that position as it's dropped to the bottom.

← ↑ Large cod require large bait and large bait requires a pennel rig.

PENNEL RIG

To bait up, the bottom hook is worked through the cuttle or squid and left with the point exposed at the bottom of the bait. Now slide the top hook down until it is level with the top of the bait. Twist the trace line round the shank three or four times and hook into the top of the bait to hold it straight. With cuttlefish, large squid and whole mackerel, large hooks of 6/0 and bigger can be used. Pennel rigs can be used for other species, baited with different baits, but the hook size needs to be reduced to suit the bait used.

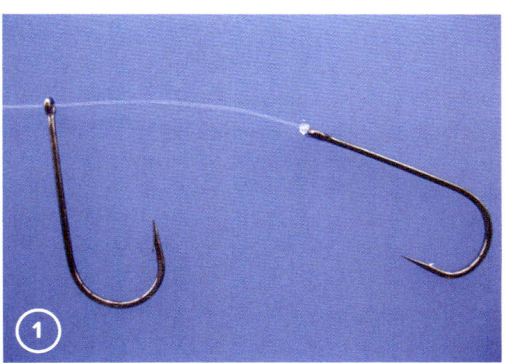

A pennel rig is made up of two hooks. Put the trace line through the eye of the first hook and slide it up the line. The second hook is tied on the end of the trace.

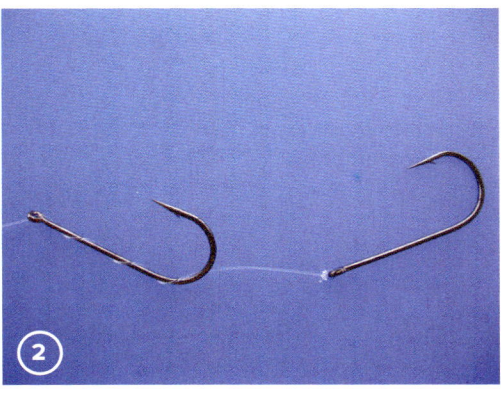

The top hook can be fixed in place a few inches above the bottom hook, but an easier method is to leave it loose and twist the trace line round the shank after the bottom hook has been baited.

RECOGNISING BITES

The best way to hook a fish is to lift the rod as the fish is biting and wind in steadily, then lift the rod firmly as you feel the weight of the fish. From this point the line should be kept tight as any slack could allow the fish to throw the hook. Wild strikes at a bite are rarely successful. Some anglers like to let the line lie across their finger to detect bites. Many fish are lost by anglers striking too quickly before the fish has got hold of the bait. One method of avoiding this is not to hold the rod but leave it propped up on the side of the boat or in a rod rest. When the fish first bites, leave it a minute or two, so that it pulls the rod tip down and swims off with the bait. In this way the fish will generally hook itself.

BITE GUIDE

Here is a guide to what the bites look and feel like for some of our more popular species.

- ▶ Bass will often show up as a tiny bite on the rod tip as they get hold of the bait, followed by a sharp pull down of the tip as they run off with it.

- ▶ Black bream bites will be seen as quick fire 'rat-a-tat-tat' pulls on the rod tip as they tear into the bait.

- ▶ Hook into a cod and there will be a steady thumping felt on the line as the fish shakes its head.

- ▶ Pouting give some sharp pulls to start with, but then come up as a dead weight usually spinning their way to the top.

- ▶ One of the most common fish that will be caught, especially when using mackerel for bait, is the lesser spotted dogfish. These will give a few good pulls on the rod to start with, but then put up little resistance and are soon brought to the surface.

- ▶ The smooth hound will sometimes run off with the bait and use its large pectoral fins to hold it in the tide, dashing about from side to side as it nears the boat.

UPTIDE FISH

One method of boat fishing we haven't touched on is uptiding. This style of fishing was developed in the shallow fast-moving waters of the Thames Estuary. It was found that more fish were caught the further from the boat the bait was, probably due to the noise in the boat magnified by the shallow water. Casting away from the boat worked with traditional weights, but the tide rolled all the leads round to the back of the boat. Grapnel and breakaway leads proved the answer as they stayed where they were cast and catches improved.

All that's required is a 6oz to 8oz grip lead, an uptide boom and a short trace. The lead is cast towards the front of the boat, but out at about 45 degrees from the boat so t doesn't go over the anchor rope. When the lead hits the water plenty of line is let out so the weight can sink to the bottom and the bow in the line allows it to grip. Bites show up as normal on the rod tip, but if a decent fish takes the bait the tip will spring up as the weight is pulled free and the fish moves downtide. If this happens wind in fast until all the slack is taken up and you can feel its weight.

⬆ Grapnel and breakaway leads are designed to hold the bottom and not allow the tide to wash the tackle downtide. On retrieval the breakaway wires spring back to allow the weight to come free of the seabed.

LANDING FISH

A landing net is required as the light tackle needed to tempt some of our most sporting fish won't allow the fish to be lifted over the side of the boat. Slipping a net under a bass, cod, mullet or big bream makes things so much easier, and if you want to return the fish alive it will survive better.

One item that is rarely used on a boat now is the gaff. At one time most fish were hooked with a gaff and dragged into the boat; thankfully this practice has all but died out as anglers are keen not to damage fish that can be released. Everyone knows the value of conservation so, if a fish is not required for eating, put it back safely so someone else can enjoy catching it when it's bigger.

← There are several reasons for using a landing net, one of the main ones being that a net allows an angler to get the fish into the boat safely.

WHAT'S THAT FISH?

CONGER EEL

While it may not be your intention to catch a conger eel there's always a chance of hooking one using any fish bait, particularly if the area is rocky or close to a reef or underwater obstruction. If the tackle is not strong enough the eel will soon find the weakness and it will spin round until it breaks the line. If one is pulled to the side of the boat, don't attempt to lift it in as it can cause mayhem with any loose items in the bottom of the boat. Instead, cut the line as close to the mouth as possible and release the eel. Any hooks, apart from stainless steel, will soon rot away and won't prevent the fish from feeding. Big eels are often caught with old rusting hooks in them that haven't stopped them from eating and from being caught again. Charter boat skippers and experienced dinghy anglers remove the hooks at the side of the boat by means of a T-bar. This is slid down the line to the bend of the hook while the trace is held tightly. The trace is then jerked downwards as the T-bar is lifted up against the bend of the hook, freeing it to allow the eel to drop back into the sea.

Small congers can be eaten and at one time were popular when baked in milk in the oven. If a conger eel is wanted for eating, it will need to be brought on board in a landing net or by pulling over using the trace. Don't attempt to get the hook out while the fish is still alive, and when you do, use a pair of pliers. The only part of the conger eel that should be eaten is between the back of the head and the vent (anus).

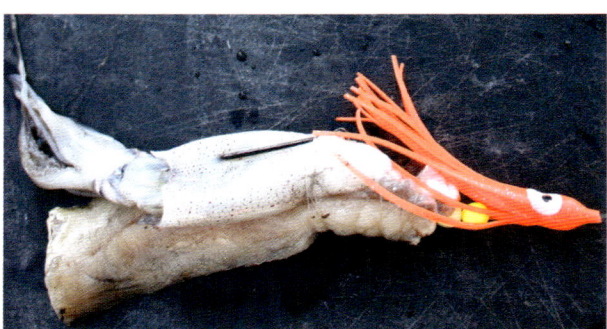

← This conger eel bait is a side of mackerel and a whole squid with a bright red muppet on the trace above.

⬆ This monster weighed in at just over 100lb. The power of a big conger is quite amazing and without specialist tackle would be virtually impossible to land.

BULL HUSS

The bull huss, or greater spotted dogfish, is generally much bigger than its cousin the lesser spotted dogfish. Apart from its overall size it has larger and far fewer spots than the lesser spotted dogfish. The nasal flaps of the bull huss (below) are well separated while the dogfish has nasal flaps that are almost or completely joined.

They can be caught on fresh mackerel, squid, sand eel and crab bait. Bull huss grow to over 20lb with the average size caught on rod and line between 5lb and 8lb. A fish of over 14lb is considered a specimen in most areas.

⬆ In the bull huss the nasal flaps form two distinct lobes.

⬆ The bull huss has a mottled appearance which helps it blend into its surroundings.

DOGFISH

The lesser-spotted dogfish, or robin huss, as they are known in some parts of the country, are widespread and can be a bit of a nuisance if they keep taking the bait intended for quality eating fish such as cod. But dogfish are very sweet to eat and benefit from having a cartilaginous structure that allows the meat to come off cleanly with no sharp bones.

The one difficulty is skinning them ready for consumption. All the fins should be cut off and a V-shape flap of skin sliced behind the head so a good grip can be made before pulling down to the tail. This should leave a long thin tube of meat that can be cut into suitable cutlets for cooking. The average dogfish caught weighs less than 2lb and the British record is just under 5lb.

⬆ Dogfish numbers are massive due to its prolific breeding behaviour.

RAYS

Although referred to as skate in fish shops, nearly all the ones caught off the UK coastline are rays. We have five species that are the most likely to be caught on light to medium tackle fished on the bottom. From the smallest upwards they are the spotted, small-eyed, undulate, thornback and blonde ray. It would be extremely rare to catch any of the other species as they are mostly found in very deep water and caught on specialist bait and tackle.

SPOTTED RAY

The spotted ray is a small species that seldom grows bigger than 8lb in weight; any fish over 5lb is considered a specimen. They can be caught on quite small hooks and bait, very often picking up strips of squid, mackerel or a ragworm intended for species such as bream.

The way to tell them apart from young blonde rays is to note how near the edge of the wings the spots finish. The blonde ray has small spots that go all the way to the edge, while the spotted ray has larger spots that finish several centimetres from the edge.

↑ The spotted ray has small thorns or prickles on either side of the eyes, on the front wing edges, down the centre, and along the length of the tail.

SMALL-EYED RAY

The small eyed ray is a very pale beige colour with faint white lines running parallel to the edge of the wings. There are often several white spots over the centre of the body. They are found along the south coast of the UK during the summer months, when they come in to spawn in areas where there is a mix of sand and boulders. Their eggs are enclosed in sachets, better known as 'mermaids' purses', with twisted tendrils at each corner so they can tangle in the weed where they will remain until the young emerge.

The small-eyed ray can grow to around 18lb but a fish over 12lb would be a specimen catch, with the average likely to be nearer 8lb. It feeds on sand eels and other small fish as well as prawns and crabs.

The eggs of small-eyed ray are enclosed in 'mermaids' purses' and take between five and seven months to develop to a fully formed ray.

Small-eyed rays spawn during the summer months along the south coast of the UK. They feed on sand eels, crabs, prawns and small fish.

UNDULATE RAY

The undulate ray seems to have become more prolific over the past decade, with several caught near the 20lb mark, the record being 21lb 4oz. The distinctive, broad brown streaks across its body make it an easy fish to identify. It can be caught on fish bait such as squid, mackerel and sometimes takes crab bait set out for bass or smooth hound.

THORNBACK RAY

The thornback ray has lots of dark and light spots across its back, but varies tremendously from area to area. A more reliable identification comes from the row of sharp thorns along its tail, which continue on to its back. The thornback is probably the most widespread ray, as it favours inshore banks and estuaries where it can find a good supply of prawns and crabs. It moves inshore early in the year when it can be caught using herring, squid and mackerel before it switches to peeler crab in spring.

It is good to eat and very easy to cook once it has been skinned. Thornbacks can grow to nearly 30lb but a fish of over 15lb is considered an excellent specimen.

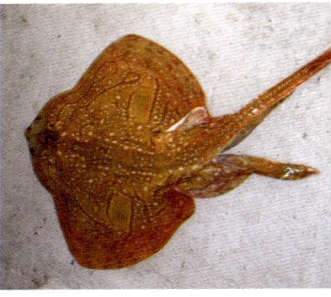

⬆ The undulate ray can be identified by the distinctive brown streaks across its body.

⬆ Adult thornback rays usually have large spines with swollen bases on their backs and sometimes on their underside.

BLONDE RAY

The blonde ray is the biggest of our resident rays, growing to around 40lb. They are very rarely caught by chance as they frequent areas where the tide rips, which means using heavy weights and strong tackle. Fishing over the slacker part of the tide with squid or mackerel bait could produce a fine specimen like the one below, which was caught from the banks off Weymouth. The majority of blonde rays are returned alive as anglers are keen to see them survive for the future.

A big blonde ray will give a good account of itself when hooked, especially if there is a strong tide running. It opens its wings and uses the tide to kite about, making it difficult to bring to the boat. They often come to the surface some distance from the boat and need strong tackle to bring them in against the tide.

The blonde ray has a short snout and the outer angles of the wings are almost right-angled. ➡

TOP TIP

Blonde rays prefer fish bait – a whole squid and a long strip of mackerel are excellent for catching this fish.

TURBOT AND BRILL

Turbot and brill can both be caught on the drift, but this is only in a few specific areas, so they are included in this section as they often caught by anglers fishing downtide from an anchored boat. Both are delicious to eat which makes them a prize catch.

The turbot is a flatfish that is almost circular, with both eyes on the right and the gill cover on the left. It lives in or around sandbanks where it ambushes sand eels and other small fish. Its back is mainly brown but it can change its colouration to imitate the surrounding seabed. The turbot's back is covered in bony lumps called tubercles. The fish can grow to over 30lb in weight.

← Brill are often caught in the same areas as turbot but are generally smaller. They are more oval in shape and have a smooth back with no bony tubercles. Brill can grow to 16lb, but a fish over 10lb would be thought a bit special.

← Note the difference in shape between the brill (above) and the turbot (left), the brill being more oval than the circular turbot.

WHITING

Although regarded as a winter fish, whiting can be caught all-year-round in deep water; they move inshore from the end of October through to March. The fish are slim-bodied with small sharp teeth that can rip off the bait quickly. As the majority of whiting are fairly small, they can be fiddly to prepare for cooking, but the white flesh is milder than cod so it's worth the effort.

Whiting grow to nearly 7lb but the average one caught is around 1lb. Those caught in Cornwall and Devon are generally larger than those caught further east in the Channel and North Sea.

⬆ Whiting can be caught using either lugworm, squid or fish bait.

TOP TIP Whiting feed off the bottom and a pasternoster rig baited with mackerel, squid or worm will catch them readily over the slack tide.

FISH IDENTIFIER

FLOAT FISHING
Increasing your catch rate

FLOAT FISHING

One of the most enjoyable styles of sea fishing is using a float. It gives a point to focus on and the excitement of seeing the float plunging beneath the surface never wanes. If the boat is at anchor, the float can be cast uptide and allowed to bob along in the current until it's some way behind the boat. With the bait dragging along the bottom, fish like flounders and plaice will be attracted. With the bait suspended in mid-water, mackerel, garfish, scad and pollack can be caught. On the bottom worms and strips of squid work best, while a sand eel or a thin strip of mackerel are the favoured bait for mid-water.

A float can be used to good effect when the boat is drifting in the tide. The float needs to be set to the fish's anticipated depth. Mackerel, garfish, pollack, mullet and scad will be found in the top couple of metres, while fish such as flatfish and bream will require the float to be set so that the bait is presented close to the bottom. By using a 4-turn stop knot (see page 52) you can slide the float up or down to the required depth. Most fish will take the float straight under and it's just a matter of lifting the rod to hook them. Some species like pollack that swim up to take the bait will lift the float so that it momentarily lies flat on the surface. Be ready for it to immediately plunge under as the fish turns and heads for the safety of the weeds or rocks. As the fish is brought to the boat the float will slide down the line to rest on the weight so the fish can be brought in easily. If the float was in a fixed position of more than two metres it would not be easy to land the fish.

Floats for the sea are generally larger for boat fishing than those used in rivers. This is to compensate for the swell in the sea and to carry more weight so that they can be cast easily.

← The excitement of seeing a float plunging beneath the surface never wanes.

SETTING UP A FLOAT

Before tying on the trace to the hook, test out the float to see if the weight is heavy enough to cock the float properly but not so much that it pulls the float under. Cast it out from the boat and watch it move downtide to see if any corrections are needed. If fishing in fairly deep water you may have to add a couple of split (or swan) lead shots half a metre from the bait to ensure the bait sinks, so take this into consideration when checking how the float lies.

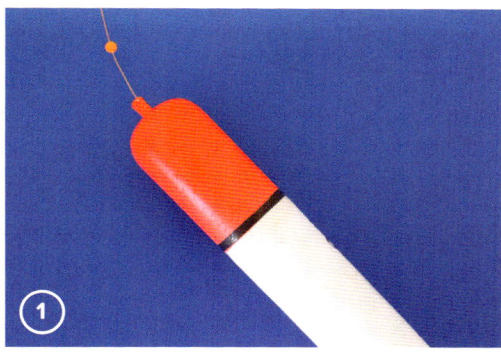

Slide a small bead up the line followed by the float.

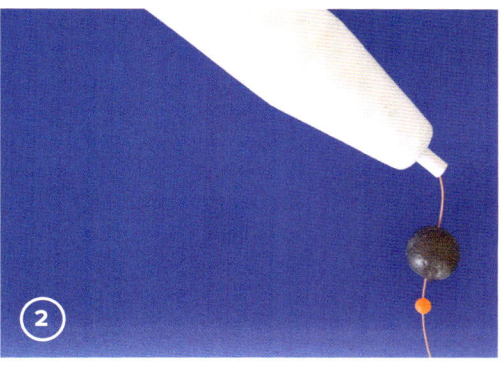

Then slide another small bead and a ball weight below the float.

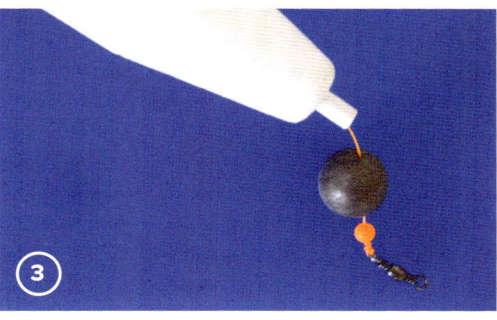

Tie a swivel on to the end of the line. Connect a trace of about one metre with a suitable hook.

WHAT'S THAT FISH?

BASS

Float fishing for bass is one of the most exciting methods of catching these silver predators. A fairly large float is required as the bait will be a small live fish. This can be a mackerel, scad, small pollack, sand eel, pout or poor cod.

Using a size 4/0 or 6/0 hook lightly hooked through the top lip allows the fish to swim naturally. The float will carry the live bait away as the boat drifts along with it. The live bait may spot a bass approaching and will signal this by moving the float about erratically. As the bass grabs the bait, the float plunges under and the fish is hooked. The pressure of pulling the float under is sufficient to hook the bass; then it's just a matter of playing it gently back to the boat. A landing net is very useful at this point.

For garfish use a light line of 12lb or less and a size 6 hook. When live baiting for bass, the line strength needs to be 20lb with a 4/0 to 6/0 hook. Above the top bead tie a four turn stop to stop the float sliding up the line.

⬆ From top to bottom: scad, mackerel and bass.

↑ A fish of this size is fun to reel in using a light float tackle.

POLLACK

Shallow fishing, with the float set to hold the bait just under the surface and using thin strips of fish bait, will bring mackerel and garfish. Generally speaking the garfish prefer the top metre or so, while the mackerel can be caught two or three metres down.

If you have no success, adjust the stop knot to drop the bait a little deeper until the fish are found. If the float is allowed to drift in close to some rocks or a cliff the chances of catching a pollack or wrasse increase.

Changing bait to ragworm will almost certainly bring bites from small wrasse, especially if the float is set a little deeper, as wrasse live around the rocks.

Pollack will feed some way off the bottom and follow the bait when it's being wound in.

FLOUNDER

If the boat is anchored or moored in an estuary then why not have fun with the flounders? The float should be set so that the hook drifts along just off the bottom. Bait up with a couple of large ragworms and it will be a magnet for flounders. Flounders are attracted to movement, and adding a silver spoon above the bait will add to the attraction. The biggest problem will be crabs, as they are very keen on ragworm as well.

The record flounder is just under 6lb, but most caught on rod and line are nearer to 1lb, although they can still provide plenty of fun on a light rod. When you catch a flounder you must then decide if you fancy eating it. Flounders can be muddy, especially the ones caught upriver, but some say the flounders caught in the mouth of a river, harbour or estuary are very pleasant.

← The flounder is an amazing fish which goes through an incredible transformation that takes it from a normal round fish at birth to a flatfish at adulthood.

WRASSE

There are several types of wrasse in UK waters, the biggest being the ballan that grows to nearly 6.6lb. They can be caught on float tackle when fished over or near rocks or a reef. The best bait is ragworm or crab.

A ballan wrasse can be difficult to catch as it will take the bait straight back to its lair amongst the rocks if allowed to.

The other species of wrasse that will take the same bait are much smaller and include the colourful cuckoo wrasse, the goldsinny, corkwing and Baillon's.

↑ The ballan is the biggest wrasse found in the UK and can range in colour from dull brown, yellow and green, through to orange and red.

 **TOP TIP**   Using ragworm as bait will almost certainly attract small wrasse.

FISHING FROM A KAYAK

The author would like to express his great thanks to Liam Faisey at www.cornishcanoes.co.uk for his help with the kayak chapter in this edition.

FISHING FROM A KAYAK

Over the past few years, the sport of kayak fishing has grown in popularity quite significantly. It's a great way to get afloat for a reasonable price, requiring no berthing or marina fees. Kayaks are lightweight, easily transportable and can be used to fish inshore marks that bigger boats can't get to. This allows you to fish in shallow water, between reefs and near obstructions such as cliffs, bridges and piers where a whole range of fish take shelter. A set of suitable paddles are needed and they require a leash to connect to the kayak so they cannot be lost overboard. Some kayaks have a pedal drive that are a great help if travelling longer trips but paddles should still be carried as back up.

GETTING STARTED

Before attempting to fish from a kayak it is important to get proper advice on all aspects of the safety issues and to be competent handling these small lightweight craft. Though no licences are required, anyone needing more information on the safety aspects of using a kayak should go on to the RNLI website (www.rnli.org) where they have comprehensive advice and arrange courses for anyone new to the sport.

⬇ Playing a fish.

We enlisted the help of kayak expert Liam Faisey of Wild Seas (www.wildseasfishing.co.uk) and Cornwall Canoes (www.cornwall-canoes.co.uk) to list the things required for a safe and properly equipped kayak.

KAYAK KIT

It is important to ensure you are equipped with all the necessary gear and safety equipment so that you can enjoy your day fishing whilst staying safe on the water.

⬆ Paddle length is important.

PADDLES

You won't get far without a paddle. This is your primary means of propulsion on a kayak, unless you have a pedal-driven kayak (see below). When choosing one, length and construction are primary. Don't buy cheap paddles as all you can expect will be something that is heavy and poorly designed. As the price increases, they become lighter, with more efficient blade constructions and shapes, making them overall nicer to use. This will see more of the energy you put into paddling transferred into pushing the kayak forwards through the water.

Paddles with fibreglass and carbon shafts (the bit you hold) combined with reinforced plastic blades are a great option and are in the £60–£150 range. They are ideal for most kayaking and offer a trade-off between price and performance. The Feelfree Day Tourer with a fibreglass shaft is a great choice in this price range. You can expect to spend £200+ for premium lightweight designs with carbon shafts and stiff composite blades. They are pricey but are a joy to use with an almost weightless feel to them. If you plan to fish regularly on the water or intend to cover longer distances lighter is best.

Paddle length is another important consideration and the best length is primarily dictated by kayak width. If your paddle is too short you'll keep hitting your hands on the side of the kayak; too long and the paddle will feel unwieldy and inefficient. At the correct length it will maximise each paddle stroke. For the vast majority of the fishing kayaks on the market a 220cm long paddle will be fine. Narrower kayaks (less than 72cm beam) may require a 215cm and wider kayaks (greater than 82cm beam) may need a 230cm. Make sure you buy a paddle leash as well, to ensure the paddle stays attached to your kayak.

PEDAL DRIVES

Many kayak manufacturers offer pedal drive kayaks, where a drive system will slot through the bottom of the hull, giving you the capability of using your legs to drive the kayak. If you are likely to be travelling long distances or spending a lot of time out on the water you will save a lot of energy using one of these systems. Most drives allow you to pedal backwards too! Conventional paddles should still be on-board as a back-up, though. Pedal drive kayaks are now the go-to option for any serious kayak angler thanks to the huge number of advantages they offer including increased speed, better performance in windy conditions, 'hands-free' trolling, precision craft positioning whilst vertical lure fishing, holding position in tide/current and much more. Pedal kayaks from Hobie are the most popular, with a number of models to suit all styles of angling.

ROOF RACKS

Unless you live right on the coast, kayaks are not the easiest objects to move around, and the best solution is to use a roof rack on the car. Don't go for cheap generic or universal racks as these are unlikely to fit your car or van properly and often have low load ratings. It's always best to buy a roof-rack system that has a car model specific fitting kit, as these will have higher load ratings of 75–100kg, offering a much safer option for transporting large kayaks.

Systems from Swedish manufacturer Thule are popular amongst kayakers and motorists alike. Specific kayak carriers can be bought to hold the hull on to the rack but, in most cases, all you need is some padding for the bars and a set of cam buckle straps. Don't use ratchet straps; they can put a lot of unnecessary tension on the hull of a kayak, potentially leading to damage.

TROLLEYS

Getting a fully loaded fishing kayak from your car to the water's edge and back is not an easy task without a kayak trolley. It's best to avoid trolleys that rely on metal uprights passing through the kayak scupper holes. The uprights can cause hull cracks to form due to the force exerted on the plastic by the posts. So go for a trolley where the

kayak sits on supportive pads. There is really only one that you will ever need to get – the Railblaza C-Tug. It has a strong plastic design that won't rust, large grippy hull pads, cam buckle straps to hold the kayak securely, is collapsible in seconds and will fit in the front hatch of most fishing kaya<s. If you ask almost any kayak angler they will recommend them.

BUOYANCY AIDS

An essential safety item for any kayaker is a buoyancy aid, known as Personal Flotation Devices (PFDs). Whilst there is no law impelling their use, it is seen as a compulsory item amongst the kayak fishing fraternity. If you become separated from your kayak in the water, a buoyancy aid will help to keep you afloat whilst you await rescue.

These are worn on the torso and contain closed-cell foam to provide buoyancy to the wearer. Don't skimp by buying a cheap buoyancy aid, your life may well rely on it at some point. Most kayak anglers opt for designs with pockets – handy for storing small items of tackle and tools. Models with a 'high-back' design are also popular. This is where the lower back section is constructed of mesh or very thin padding with the buoyancy concentrated at the top of the back, so as not to interfere with high back rests often used on fishing kayaks. The most popular option for kayak anglers is the Palm Kola Angler, offering plenty of comfort and with functional storage for safety items and tackle.

OTHER SMALL SAFETY ITEMS

With fishing lines, anchoring lines and leashes on the kayak, the risk for entanglement during a capsize situation is quite high. Always carry a rescue knife attached to your buoyancy aid and make sure it's in an easy-to-reach position so that you can cut yourself free if you do get tangled in the water. Look for blunt-ended knife designs so that you can't accidentally stab yourself, one with a stainless-steel blade and one-hand operated sheath for easy access. Rope cutters are good to have too. These hooked blades are razor sharp and will cut through lines and rope with ease. The Beaver Trigger Line Cutter is an excellent example. Many kayakers would always carry a whistle, preferably a pea-less design as they work even when wet. These are useful for attracting the attention of others at close range.

It is also worth mentioning flares. There are mixed views on their use as they rely on someone seeing the flare and then also alerting the rescue services for you. They're really only useful to aid someone looking for you. Don't rely solely on them, but they are a useful extra.

COMMUNICATION

It's always a good idea to have the capability to contact the shore. It is essential if you are kayak fishing alone. When things go wrong, as they sometimes do, and you find yourself in a difficult situation, you need to be in a position to contact someone who can help you.

MOBILE PHONES

As a bare minimum carry a mobile phone in a dry pouch although, if you have ever tried using a touchscreen phone with wet hands, you will know that water and touch control do not always work well together! If you have a smartphone, make sure you know how to activate the voice-controlled assistant (such as Siri on Apple iPhones, activated by saying 'Hey Siri') so that you can vocally initiate an emergency call. This may be the only way you can operate your phone when in the water. The downside to relying on a mobile phone is that not all areas have good signal reception, especially close to cliffs and low hills.

VHF RADIOS

Most regular kayak anglers will carry a handheld VHF radio on their buoyancy aid, providing a direct means of contact with the Coastguard, and other water users, via channel 16. Look for floating units with at least an IPX7 waterproof rating and output wattage of 5 or 6W, with a 1W low power mode. You will need to buy a good quality unit, with models from ICOM and Standard Horizon being most widely used amongst kayakers.

More expensive models will have a function called Digital Selective Calling (DSC) with integrated GPS. DSC has a few uses but most importantly it allows you to send out a distress signal to other DSC users (including the Coastguard) incorporating your GPS location, at the push of a button. This transmits an 'I need urgent help and I'm in this position' message to potential rescuers. You require two licences for a VHF radio; one to own the radio, which is available free from Ofcom, and one to transmit VHF signals. On the course you will be taught to use a VHF with confidence and speak to other users using the correct protocols. Once you have it, your operator's certificate lasts a lifetime.

PLBS (PERSONAL LOCATOR BEACONS)

Many kayakers carry Personal Locator Beacons (PLBs) – they act as an additional method of sending a distress signal and GPS location to rescue services. PLBs transmit signals via satellite and have global coverage. Press a button on a PLB anywhere in the world and the emergency services will be sent to your location.

CLOTHING

Dress for immersion. The sea temperatures around the UK are cold in the winter and only a bit less cold in the summer. As a minimum you should wear a wetsuit or neoprene leggings and top. These can get a little sticky in warm weather but offer an inexpensive clothing option for kayak fishing. On cooler days put on a cagoule to cut out the wind chill.

The safest and warmest option is a surface immersion dry-suit, paired up with appropriate base layers depending on the weather. This is a good option for all but the hottest days in summer when things may get a little warm. A good quality breathable dry suit, with built in fabric socks, convenience zip and comfortable glide-skin neoprene neck seal will set you back upwards of £500. There are also 'two-piece' clothing options with various dry pant and cagoule combos available, which allow further flexibility dependant on the weather and conditions. A specialist kayak shop is your best bet for getting suited and booted with suitable clothing.

← A seat can make sitting in the same position for hours more comfortable.

COMFORT

What you sit on aboard the kayak is important as spending several hours on the sea can make for a sore behind if there is not sufficient cushioning. There are loads of clip-in seat designs available as well as some that have a back support, which can prove valuable after an hour or two sitting in the one position.

TECHNIQUES

LURE FISHING

One of the most popular fish to go for from the kayak are bass. Paddling along with a lure trailing some ten to twenty yards behind the kayak will produce an aggressive bite as the bass takes the lure. On light tackle the bass will give the angler plenty to think about as it dives for shelter. This method will also produce other species such as pollack, mackerel and garfish. Some of the most popular lures for trolling are Deep Divers which will work at 10-25ft+ depending on how fast you troll, but a whole array of soft plastic lures with weighted jig heads also work well while trolling (see page 59).

↑ Deep Diver lures.

⬆ Drift fishing.

LIVE BAIT

Fishing close into a reef will give access to the many small fish that seek shelter there. Use a sabiki rig to catch joey mackerel and sand eels that can then be used for live baiting for bass. They need to be put in a small bucket with an aerator to keep them alive. The live bait can then be fished under a float on a size 2/0 to 4/0 hook, depending on the size of the bait. Check the depth and set the float to keep the live bait a few feet from the bottom to avoid snagging up and losing tackle. Allow the kayak to drift close to the reef so that the bass can ambush the live bait as it swims by.

FISH FOR THE POT

The easiest way to catch fish to eat is to drift across the sand banks with a light weight and a flowing trace baited with lugworm or ragworm. This method can produce plaice, flounder and dab along with the odd gurnard, whiting and even codling. While it's not recommended to eat flounders, all the rest are excellent, the gurnard being a particular favourite of many fish eaters. All you do is drop the tackle down to the bottom using a 2 to 4oz weight and feel it bumping along over the sand as you drift along. A bite will register as a sharp pull on the rod tip as the fish chase after the bait, and they usually hook themselves.

FISHERMAN'S CALENDAR

When to fish

MONTH BY MONTH GUIDE

Is there a good time or bad time to fish? Not really, but most fish will avoid feeding in the strongest of tides. On very big tides when the current is at its most powerful, the best time to fish is from one-and-a-half hours before the top of the tide until a similar time on the ebb. Fish cannot afford to spend too much time battling against strong tides and will lie close to the seabed, behind reefs, wrecks or even buried under sand or gravel to save energy.

Experience has shown that when the tides are strong, the fish move closer to shore to feed, and move offshore on the neap tides when the flow is less powerful. Many people favour night-time fishing, but in practice there is often more action at dusk, before it settles down again in the night. Sunrise can also see more activity, particularly with fish like bass that use the half-light to ambush their prey. The seasons play a big part in deciding which fish are around and there are specific times when certain species are more prolific.

As a basic guide, in the winter you will catch mainly whiting and cod. Spring will provide plaice, thornbacks and smooth hound. Summer will bring the mackerel, bass, bream, pouting, rays and tope. Autumn is a mixture of the summer species and the first of the whiting and then it's back to winter fishing again. Over the next few pages you will find a more detailed month by month guide of what species to expect.

JANUARY

At the beginning of the year, fishing is generally in the doldrums. The cod season is coming to an end, but there are still some good ones to be had. The whiting start thinning out this month, but flounders make their way inshore to harbours and estuaries. Some years there's a good run of dabs. This small flatfish is in its prime early in the year and they are one of the sweetest of fish to eat. Pouting and dogfish always seem to be around.

FEBRUARY

February is definitely the worst time of year as far as small boat fishing is concerned. Inshore, the only things stirring are dogfish and thornbacks, with a smattering of whiting still hanging around. One of the best baits for thornbacks early in the year is a chunk of herring. For the bigger boats, charter boats and any large private craft, the pollack in mid-channel can be superb, as this is when they are at their largest before spawning.

Drift over wrecks using an artificial eel such as a Red Gill, sidewinder, Eddystone or a storm shad, on a two or three metre long trace. Let the lure down to the bottom, then slowly wind up 30 turns of the reel. Repeat the process until a pollack follows the lure, grabs it and heads back to the wreck. After this initial dive, play it carefully back to the boat.

⬆ A period of sharp frosts encourages the dab's appetite and they can't resist the lugworm.

MARCH

There's always room for optimism in March, with plaice starting to show over mussel beds and sandbanks as they return from spawning. The plaice will be thin to start with but soon build up body weight. A run of spring codling is always on the cards but cannot be guaranteed.

If it's been a warmish winter the first of the bream come into spawn at the end of the month.

Using fish bait on the bottom can pick up spur dogfish at this time of the year and off Scotland for most of the year. They are similar to tope and smooth hound in that they look like a grey shark, but watch out for the two sharp spines on their back, just in front of the dorsal fins.

⬆ Peeler crabs are terrific bait in April. They can be found at low tide hiding under weed or in old car tyres, tin cans or anywhere they can hide away until their shell hardens.

APRIL

In April boat angling really hots up. There are lots of plaice around and the first of the smooth hounds come in looking for the early peeler crabs. It's the peeler crabs that get things going, as bass will be hunting them down as well.

Peeler crabs are crabs that are in the process of shedding their shell to allow them to grow. While in this state they are vulnerable to most species of fish and give out a strong scent making them very effective bait. They can be found hiding under seaweed in rock pools and around the base of groynes exposed at low tide. In estuaries they can be found in the mud under anything that offers a bit of protection such as old tin cans, slates and car tyres.

Black bream make a welcome re-appearance this month and on the sandbanks the first of the turbot and brill will be found along with plaice that are now beginning to fill out.

MAY

May is one of the peak months of the season with all sorts of rays, wrasse, plaice, smooth hounds, tope and congers around. The mating male bream will have a blue hue to them through this month. Much of this action is because the first of the mackerel have arrived.

Bass switch from feeding on crab to mackerel, so live baiting will start to be productive. Wreck fishing really kicks off with the cod and pollack in peak condition. Lead heads, jellyworms, storm shads, sidewinders and Red Gill evolutions are all effective for these species.

↑ This male bream is in full mating colours, clearly showing a blue hue around its head.

 **TOP TIP** Early spring is a good time to drift for plaice with lugworm or ragworm, tipped off with long, thin strips of squid.

↑ The smooth hound prefers sandy gravel bottoms as its main habitat, where it can find plenty of crustaceans to eat.

JUNE

The mackerel shoals arrive in big numbers which spark off some super fishing with bass being a particular favourite for the next few months. Black bream have spread right along the UK south coast by now and there are smooth hounds, rays, topes, bull huss, congers and wrasse to be had.

Smooth hounds can be confused with small tope, but a glance at the teeth will easily confirm which is which. The tope has sharp meat-eating teeth, like sharks, while the crab-eating smooth hound has a flat crushing type of mouth.

JULY

The fishing continues to be excellent through July, with large rays a feature from some points off the Isle of Wight through to Weymouth. Big blonde rays up to 30lb will be caught on the banks where the tides run fast. All the regular species continue to be caught, with mackerel the most universal bait.

Smooth hound fishing hits a peak with peeler crab, hermit crab and squid the top bait. Drifting with baited mini shrimps and hokkai lures at this time of the year will catch some nice bream and gurnard (right).

AUGUST

There's little change, with plenty of fish to be caught. For some really fun fishing, try float fishing with a thin strip of mackerel or a sand eel. You could hook a garfish that will take some spectacular leaps out of the water when hooked.

Late in the month the trigger fish begin to make an appearance, and every year there seem to be more and more of these hard fighting and extremely tasty fish. Another fish that will be moving north into British waters is the gilt head bream, along with its cousin the red bream. Neither of these fish is prolific, but they still remain a likelihood in certain areas of the south-west.

With the better weather and long days, anglers can put in plenty of time fishing, and will be rewarded with numerous different species.

⬆ The tub gurnard is one of the many species that can be caught on hokkai lures.

SEPTEMBER

This month is probably the best of the year for fishing, as the summer fish are still around and the first of the winter species start moving in. Most of the fish like the flatfish that spawned early in the year are now in peak condition.

Congers are feeding well on the wrecks and bass will be patrolling the reefs feeding on mackerel and scad. Black bream and smooth hound will be feeding up before moving offshore. There's also plenty of ray, the first of the cod, anc mackerel are still around in big numbers. Trigger fish will now be well established on certain hot spots and should stay until early October.

OCTOBER

Male cuckoo wrasse (below) are one of the most spectacular fish likely to be caught in UK waters. In comparison to the bright blue and orange of the male, the female is a pale orange with three dark spots on the back just in front of the tail.

Winter fish will be moving in, with a run of whiting, followed closely by the cod. Mackerel and bream will thin out as the month goes on, but bass will be around all month. The wrecks will still be producing conger, pollack and cod. Turbot and brill will still be feeding on sand eels over the banks.

This is the month when just about anything can turn up, and catches can often be made up of summer and winter species in equal numbers.

⬇ The male cuckoo wrasse is one of the most spectacular fish likely to be caught in the UK.

NOVEMBER

In most areas cod fever affects the sea angler, as there's the best chance of landing one from fairly close inshore at this time of the year. Whiting and dogfish will often clean off bait in no time, but use several squid on a large hook or switch to cuttlefish to prevent this, giving the cod a better chance of finding the bait. Large squid bait is often picked up by conger eels at this time of the year, even on open ground. Congers are very sensitive to the cold weather and tend to pack on weight now and feed very little over the next couple of months.

TOP TIP

Make sure you choose some quality thermal clothes to keep out the wet and cold as you might encounter some harsh conditions.

DECEMBER

Time to break out the thermals and warm jackets as the fishing slows up. The main target in December is cod, with whiting always competing for the bait. A couple of nice cod and a bucket of reasonably-sized whiting can make fishing in December well worthwhile.

Early in the month congers often leave the wrecks and feed up before going into a partial hibernation, as they are badly affected by cold weather. In the big freeze of 1962/63 hundreds of dead conger eels were found along our shores, caught out by the extreme cold.

⬆ December is the month to dress up warm and put down big squid bait for cod.

FURTHER AFIELD

Travelling away from home

GOING SOUTH

Many boat owners cruising out of UK waters will be heading past the Channel Islands along the Atlantic coast of France. Some may push down the coast of Portugal and Spain to reach Gibraltar and the Mediterranean. The possibilities for fishing while trolling and at overnight stops are excellent and will give a chance to find ever more exotic fish as boats travel further south. The Channel Islands are difficult to navigate but enjoy some brilliant fishing. Trolling for bass can produce fish well into double figures using some of the lures shown earlier in the book. Drifting over the sandbanks with strips of mackerel, garfish or sand eels on long traces and fishing on the bottom will find turbot and brill.

Down the coast of France the species will be similar to those caught in our home waters, and fishing at anchor will produce pouting, flatfish, conger, bass and gurnard, but there will be more bream and trigger fish when bottom fishing. Trolling will produce mackerel, garfish, Spanish mackerel and the first of the skipjack tuna could even be landed.

⬆ A double figure dentex bream can be a real handful on light tackle.

⬆ The further south you travel the more likely it is that a barracuda will hit your bait.

From Portugal south there will be even more species of bream, with as many as 15 different types possible, some of them, such as the dentex bream, growing to double figures. The more exotic fish will also be in evidence, with a trolled lure likely to be taken by bonito, skipjack tuna, dorado or barracuda. Make sure your reels are fully loaded with line, as all of these species are easily capable of running off 100m of line and will give you some serious fun getting them back to the boat and on board. The adventurous skipper taking his boat into the Mediterranean will find the fishing harder because of the clear water and the lack of fish, which is possibly due to sustained over fishing.

OTHER SPECIES

DORADO

Fishing down the Atlantic coast of Europe as far as Gibraltar will provide the opportunity to catch some of the more exotic fish found in these waters. Trolling a lure could produce a strike from a brilliantly coloured dorado (dolphin fish – below). They hunt in packs and will attack lures in very aggressive fashion. They are also delicious to eat and go well on a barbecue. If a dorado is hooked it's worth circling around and trying again in the same area, as they travel in small shoals and will follow a hooked fish right to the boat on occasions. They are brilliant fighters – they will tail-walk and put up a stiff resistance when hooked. The superb colours of green and yellow soon fade after they have been out of the water for some time. Dorado are a fast-growing fish, achieving weights of 8lb to 11lb within a couple of years.

⇩ Dorado are a striking looking fish that fight hard and are delicious to eat.

BARRACUDA

Another aggressive predator that will be interested by a lure trolled behind the boat is the barracuda. The biggest problem here is their very sharp teeth, which are likely to bite off the lure. A short piece of wire line to the lure will prevent sharks and barracuda from getting away, but the lure will be chewed to bits anyway. As a rule it is best not to eat barracuda. Some are OK but others are toxic, so it's best to avoid them as there are plenty of other options for food. They can be caught on all sorts of lures, small fish and strips of bait. They need to be handled with care as can be seen by the set of teeth on the fish below. They are very similar in shape and power to our freshwater pike, but grow much bigger, with fish of 44lb fairly common in some parts of the world. They rarely achieve such weights down the coast of Spain and Portugal.

TOP TIP

Watch out for bird activity as this usually indicates the whereabouts of bait fish being chased by the larger predators below.

Treat the barracuda with care; those teeth are lethal.

TRIGGER FISH

At anchor, the chance of catching trigger fish becomes more likely the further south you trave , and there will be any number of different species of bream including the two-banded bream, red bream, dentex, gilthead, pandora and saddled bream. All these bream and the trigger fish make good eating aside from the fun of catching them. A longer rod with a fixed spool reel is the way to tackle these species as it allows them to show their speed and fighting qualities. Bait can be strips of frozen squid, mackerel or even cooked prawns if that's all that's available.

⬆ There is a variety of trigger fish, many of which are brightly coloured with distinctive markings.

⬆ Skipjack tuna have bold lines along their backs and sides.

SKIPJACK TUNA

Skipjack tuna can be found in vast shoals feeding on small fish – you will see the water boiling and small fish leaping to escape. These are the areas to aim for if trolling a lure, as the tuna will grab anything while in this feeding frenzy. There may also be larger predators lurking below, drawn to the commotion on the surface.

Skipjacks of just a few pounds will give good sport, running powerfully away from the boat and will take some getting in. It goes without saying what a delicious meal they make if you are lucky enough to land one. It's quite likely that some other small members of the tuna family will take the lure too. The albacore is similar to the skipjack but doesn't have stripes down the side. They are caught in large numbers in the Bay of Biscay so it's worth leaving a trolling rod out all the time in case you steam past a shoal. The other likely catch is the bonito, easily confused with the skipjack, but the lines on its back are confined to above the lateral line, while the skipjack has bold lines on its back and below the lateral line.

RED MULLET

Red mullet are caught occasionally in the UK but are prolific further south. They feed on the bottom using two long barbels that protrude below the jaw to feel out shrimps and other small creatures. As the name suggests, the fish are red but have three distinct yellow bars along the flanks. Red mullet are another very tasty fish provided they are big enough, as the average mullet caught is under a pound in weight. Despite their name they are not related to the grey mullet, but are in the same group as the goat fish. Red mullet are rarely specfically fished for, but are usually caught on bait targeting something else.

⬆ Red mullet makes a tasty meal provided they are big enough.

↑ The harbours in Portugal and Spain are full of the hard-fighting grey mullet.

GREY MULLET

All harbours hold big stocks of grey mullet, which can provide hours of fun trying to tempt them into taking a small piece of bread on a tiny hook. Try using a piece of crust, free-lined with no weight or float, and watch as the fish take it off the surface. If the fish are very shy then use a float with about a metre of line to the hook. Pinch a piece of fresh bread on to a size 6 hook, fix a split shot on to the line to take the bait down slowly and be ready for the float to plunge under. Grey mullet are considered one of the hardest fish to land because such fine tackle is required to tempt them to take the bait.

OTHER SPECIES

While sailing south from the UK watch out for a single fin flapping on the surface. Venture closer and you could find it's a large sunfish feeding on algae. These strange looking fish appear to be in distress but this is normal behaviour. If startled, the sunfish will straighten up and plunge powerfully down into the depths of the ocean. Dolphins will appear from time to time and will play just under the bow of the boat, enjoying the turbulence found there. You may spot a large turtle the further south you travel. There's a possibility blue sharks will take trolled lures and a variety of fish bait while on the drift.

There are a few other species that can be hooked almost anywhere, and these include the dragonet, bullhead, lumpsucker and bogue. None is dangerous, but the best rule of thumb is, if you can't identify it, treat it with care as it might have sharp spikes or spines so better to be on the safe side. Baiting with fish bait in Spain, Gibraltar and anywhere in the Mediterranean can produce one of the many species of grouper. They are deep-bodied fish that will test your tackle. The stone bass falls into this general group and, as its main diet consists of pollack, there's always a chance of hooking one if fishing near wrecks off the Channel Islands and French coast.

⬇ Dolphins love to swim right under the bow of a boat.

🐟 All the fish in the jack family put up a tremendous fight when hooked.

fish-identifier-page-number

JACKS

As you get nearer to Gibraltar the possibility of hooking one of the jack family increases. They are a deep-bodied species and some of them grow very large. The ones caught in this area will mostly be on the small side, but they should not be underestimated as they fight particularly well, pound for pound. Crevalle jack is the one most likely to be encountered the nearer you get to Gibraltar. In the Mediterranean, other members of the jack family such as the pilot fish, the guelly jack and the blue runner are more likely to be hooked.

GOING NORTH

Although most sailors will travel south looking for the sun, some will head north to Scotland for the wonderful scenery and the chance to sail or cruise in the deep water lochs. While most of the fish further north are similar to the rest of the UK, there are a few extras that will give good sport and make excellent eating as well.

Other fish found in Scottish waters are the common skate that grow to 200lb. They are found in the deep water of the lochs, but specialist tackle and know-how are needed to catch them. Watch out for signs offering charter trips for skate fishing and give it a try. The skate don't fight as such, but are difficult to land as they take some getting up off the bottom. Spur dogfish can be found in big shoals, while the black-mouthed dogfish is another species found in these deep waters.

COALFISH

The coalfish, or saithe, as they are known north of the border, is very similar to pollack but on close inspection the lateral line is straight, while on the pollack it forms an arch over the pectoral fin. The coalfish has a dark green back and the lateral line is white. Pollack are more of a bronze colour and the lateral line is dark. Coalfish can be caught on lures or bait and are sometimes found in vast shoals. Hokkai lures are probably the best option and they should be fished on the drift, as much of the water is too deep for anchoring.

← Coalfish can be identified by their dark green back and straight, white lateral line.

REDFISH

One of the more exotic fish that can be caught north of the border and right up into Norway are the redfish. They are often referred to as Norway haddock and prefer deep, cold water. They can become a bit of a pest, similar to pouting further south, as they will pick up bait aimed at bigger and more sporting species.

⬆ Redfish can be caught north of the border and right up into Norway.

HADDOCK

The other notable species to be found in greater numbers the further north you go are the very popular haddock. Although not as plentiful as they once were, there are still enough around to be worth fishing for. Again, drift fishing is best using a two-hook paternoster baited with mackerel, squid or shellfish.

WOLF FISH

One of the more exotic fish that can be caught off the Scottish coast is the wolf fish. This ugly looking species has extremely strong jaws and a set of crushing teeth as it lives on crabs, molluscs and sea urchins. Removing a hook from a wolf fish is best done with a disgorger or a pair of pliers. It does make for nice eating though, so it's well worth the effort. They can grow to over 22lb but the average in Scottish waters is nearer 4.4lb.

⬆ The haddock has a distinctive black spot behind the pectoral fin.

Wolf fish have very powerful jaws for crushing shellfish. ➡

WRECK FISHING
Drifting for cod and pollack

WRECK FISHING

In the waters around the UK there are thousands of wrecks made up of warships, cargo boats, trawlers, barges, submarines and aircraft. All of them will have fish living in or around them, especially during the summer months. It's well worth stopping over one of the wreck marks shown on the Admiralty Charts and having a few drifts, as the rewards can be very worthwhile. Cod are one of the species that hang around wrecks as there is always a good supply of crabs and shoals of small fish, like the pouting, using the wreckage as shelter from the strong tides and predators. Above the wrecks there will probably be pollack that feed in mid-water on the small fish such as sprat, sand eel and mackerel. Both cod and pollack eaten fresh will be well worth the effort of stopping to drift over the wreck a few times.

↑ Chartplotters will show wrecks and tide tables.

FINDING THE WRECK

When planning a trip, look to see if your journey will take you close to any wrecks and maybe include them as a waypoint, giving yourself a bit of time to fish over the top of them. Admiralty Charts show all the wrecks and underwater obstructions and these can easily be located using a GPS plotter. Not all wrecks are exactly where they are marked on the chart, but they will be pretty close. Start where the wreck is indicated on the chart then, keeping a close watch on the sonar, work the area up to 100m surrounding it until some wreckage is located. As soon as you find it, mark it on the GPS chart. With this fixed point the wreck can be sounded all round to see how large it is and which way it lies on the seabed. The next thing to do is to see which way the tide is running by steering uptide a few hundred yards before cutting the engine, then see if you drift back over the wreck. Leave the tracking mode on the GPS so you can retrace your steps if you've got it right, or use the tracking to guide you on to the right drift.

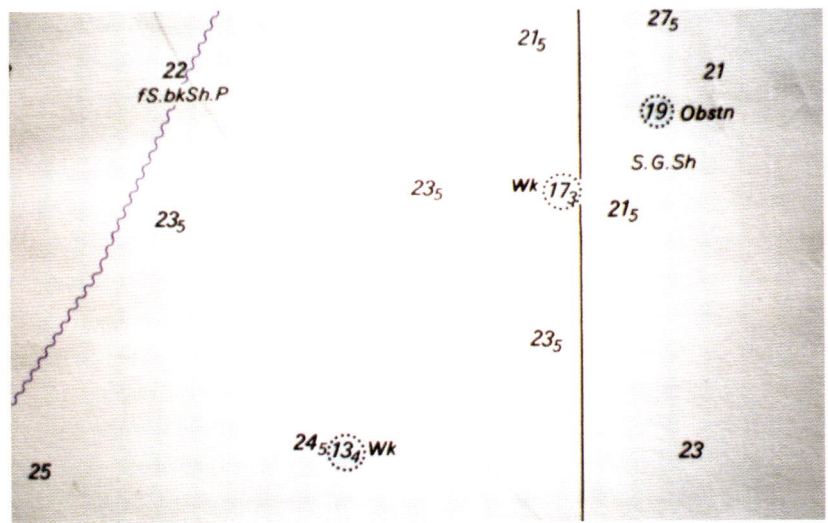

⬆ The two wrecks and the obstruction shown on the chart will all hold fish.

BEST TIDE

Fishing a wreck is best done when the tide is not at its strongest, and as a rough guide an hour and a half before and after high tide or low tide are the best. In the full run of the tide it will only be a matter of seconds before the boat has drifted over the wreck. In the period either side of high and low tide the drift won't be too strong, which will give you more time to fish it effectively.

Check the tide tables to see if it is a spring or neap tide as this will also affect the speed of the drift and catch rate. Most GPS systems will show a graph with the size of the tides on it. On a neap tide it's possible to fish wrecks more or less anytime, but the full run of spring tides will make the drift too fast for effective fishing. Generally the best fishing will be when the boat is moving at between half and one and a half knots. When it gets to over two knots the catch rate drops dramatically.

TOP TIP

Always allow for the wind when planning a drift.

COD

One of the main targets when wreck fishing will be the cod, as they use the wreck to shelter from the full run of the tide and begin to feed as the tide eases. Their diet consists of crabs, brittle star, prawns and any small fish they locate.

They will generally be found close to the bottom, but not exclusively. Many are hooked when winding up between 10 and 15 turns off the bottom. Drifting over different parts of the wreck is important as the cod will sometimes be located some way behind the wreck, close in to the wreckage and at other times they shoal above it. Once they have been located the drift can be shortened and repeated to go over the same spot.

⬆ The British record cod caught off Whitby weighed 58lb 6ozs, but hook into a fish over 10lbs and you will certainly have an exciting tussle on your hands.

 **TOP TIP**   You will feel a series of heavy nods on the rod as the cod shakes its head in an effort to dislodge the hook.

COD RIG

A cheap and easy-to-make rig for cod involves using just one swivel link:

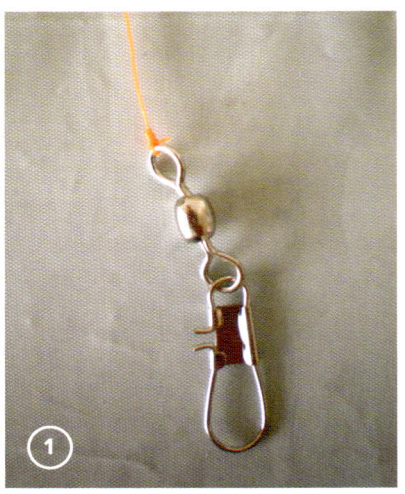

Tie the main link to the top of a swivel.

Connect the weight to the link.

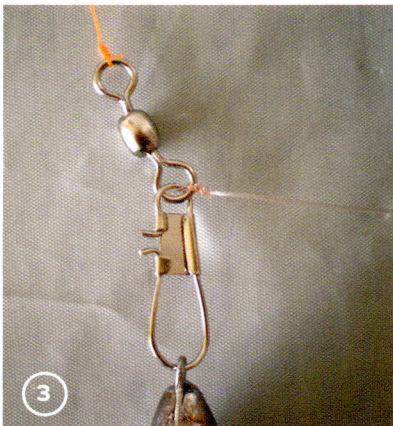

Tie the trace to the bottom of the swivel.

There is nothing complicated about fishing a wreck, as rigs are fairly basic. For the cod, a lead weight of 8oz to 12oz is needed to get hard on the bottom, so the lure can be worked in the first few feet of the seabed where the fish will most likely be. The trace line to the lure should be between one and two metres of 30lb nylon monofilament or fluorocarbon. The fluorocarbon line is more expensive than premium mono, but is meant to be virtually invisible under water.

As most wrecks are in deep water the chance of a thin piece of nylon putting the fish off is very unlikely. A slightly longer trace can be used on the bigger tides as they are not so likely to tangle, and a slightly shorter trace can be used as the tide eases. The lure can be a shad, sidewinder or artificial eel fixed to the end of the trace. The rig can be tied using just one swivel link with a weight on the bottom and the trace tied to the bottom end of the swivel.

Cod will take lures of almost any colour but do seem to have a preference for orange. It's always worth trying different colours and different sized lures as it depends what the fish are feeding on that day.

Examples of nylon and fluorocarbon lines. →

METHOD FOR COD

Stop the boat a couple of hundred yards upstream of the wreck, and drop the lure down right to the bottom. Lift the rod right up and drop it down again in a regular motion so the lead bumps along the seabed. The noise of the weight attracts the cod and they grab the shad following along behind.

When a cod is hooked it may feel like the line has caught in the bottom or on the wreck itself. After a few seconds the rod will start to thump up and down as the cod shakes its head and starts to swim off. The fish is then brought up with a pumping action on the rod, winding in the line as the rod is lowered each time.

Another way to fish the lure is to hit the bottom, then slowly wind up about ten turns of the reel. If nothing grabs the lure, drop it down again and repeat the process until a fish is hooked.

Watch the sonar as the boat drifts close to the wreck and when it first starts to show on the screen, warn everyone to wind up off the bottom to avoid hooking the wreck. It's inevitable that some tackle will be lost, so before fishing get several rigs ready to have replacements to hand.

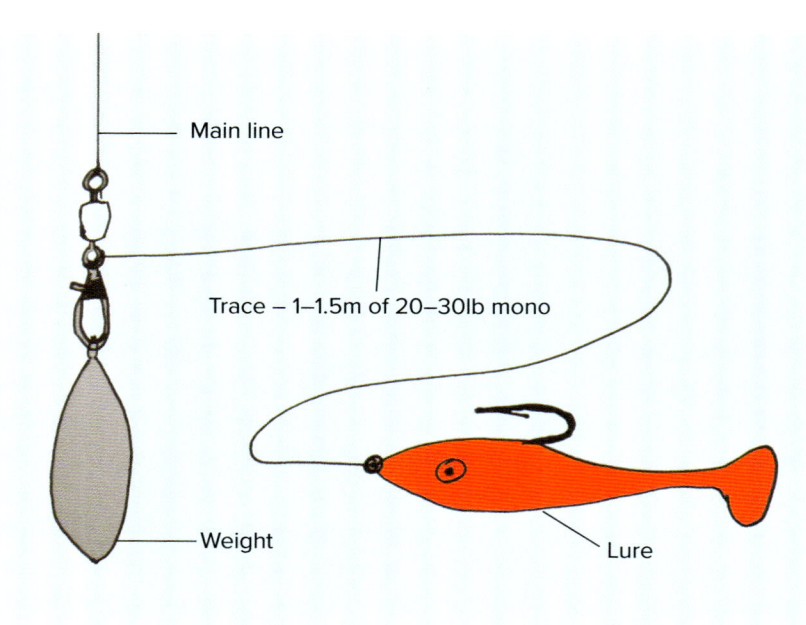

Main line

Trace – 1–1.5m of 20–30lb mono

Weight

Lure

↑ Example of a cod rig.

↑ There are a variety of cod lures that are proven 'fish takers'. The larger cod work in among the wreck picking off the smaller fish. This means they are not so bothered about the size of the lure, taking whatever comes their way.

POLLACK

The other target when wreck fishing is the pollack, one of the most underrated fish in the sea. They are in the same family as the cod, grow quite large, are good to eat and super fun to catch. Where the cod are generally located close to the bottom, the pollack patrol the water above the wreck and are often caught in mid water.

Pollack are a striking bronze colour when first caught and can be identified by their lower jaw that juts out past the upper jaw. This design of the mouth helps them seize fish when attacking from beneath. Pollack are common all round the coast of the UK, with the larger fish frequenting wrecks and deep water reefs, while the smaller and immature ones can be caught from the rocky shoreline.

⬆ The current record for the pollack is 27lb, but fish of 3lb to 12lb are the most likely to be encountered through the summer. The bigger fish are usually caught during the winter when the fish are full of roe.

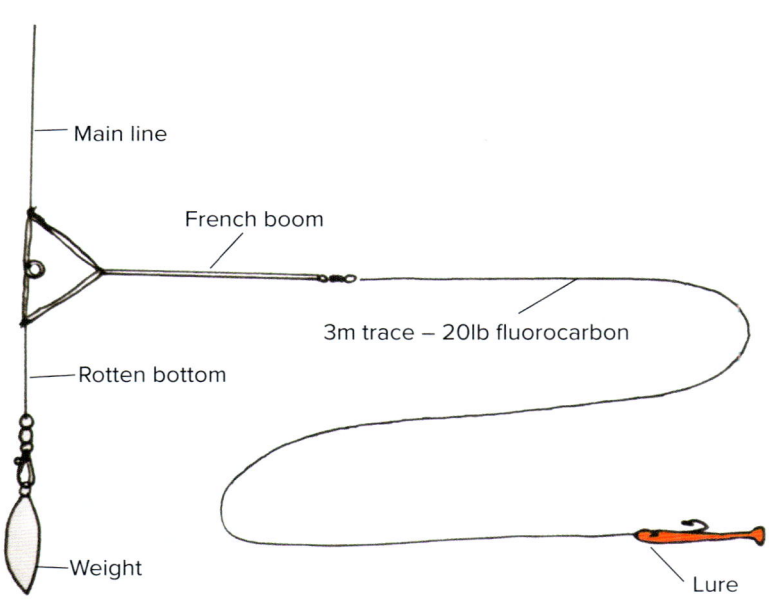

Main line

French boom

3m trace – 20lb fluorocarbon

Rotten bottom

Weight

Lure

⬆ Example of a pollack rig.

POLLACK RIG

A pollack rig is a little different from the one preferred for cod as a longer trace is generally used. To cope with the longer trace a fixed, or French, boom is used to help avoid tangles as it keeps the trace away from the main line while it's being lowered to the bottom. This method is usually referred to as a 'flying collar'. Tie the main line directly to the top of the boom – don't use a swivel link as it will slip around on the metal boom and cause tangles. On the bottom of the boom tie a short piece of nylon of about 10cm with a lead link on the end. This should be slightly less than breaking strain to the main line as it needs to break off if the bottom is snagged. This is referred to as a 'rotten bottom' and another way to do it is to use an elastic band to hold the lead as the band can spring the weight clear if snagged, or break off if firmly caught. A trace of between two and four metres of 20lb fluorocarbon or nylon is used depending on the strength of tide. As the tide slackens the trace may need shortening as it will be more liable to tangles. An artificial sand eel or a jellyworm is then attached to the end of the trace. Favourite colours for pollack are black, black with a red tail and dark red.

METHOD

Catching pollack is one of the more skilful and enjoyable parts of sea fishing, and will frustrate and satisfy the angler in almost equal measure. Once again the boat should be stopped a few hundred yards upstream of the wreck and the lines lowered to the bottom. The line should then be wound up slowly and the number of turns counted up to around 30. If no fish are felt by this time, let the lure back to the bottom and start again. When you feel a pull on the line keep slowly winding and the rod tip will pull over as the pollack starts to dive. Don't strike but keep winding steadily and the fish will hook itself and then it will need pumping to the surface.

⬆ That initial dive of a pollack is one of the most exciting things a sea angler experiences. A big portion of their diet is made up of sand eels, so using the artificial plastic sand eels (above) rather than the chunkier shads that the cod enjoy is probably the best option.

Bass will attack any coloured lures. ➡

BASS

One of the other fish that can be caught over wrecks is also the most striking looking fish in the sea: the bass. With its bold silvery scales and impressive spiny fins that stand erect when first caught, it is probably the favourite fish to catch for the majority of sea anglers. Their take is very aggressive as they are often competing with other bass for the same bait. They can be caught on most coloured lures, but seem to have a liking for pearl, white, and blue and white.

They are a fish that can easily be fluked and it's on the first couple of drifts they are mostly caught. By the time the boat has been over the wreck a few times they seem to disappear. Professional bass anglers will go to great lengths to make a wide berth of the wreck when they go up to start another drift so they don't put them off the feed. To catch a bass over a wreck, a better method is to firstly catch a mackerel on feathers and put it on live. With the mackerel hooked on to a 6/0, it is dropped to the bottom then wound up four or five turns of the reel and held there. Bass will find it hard to resist.

PREPARING AND COOKING FISH

Top tips for making the most of your catch

PREPARING FISH

As soon as a fish is caught and brought into the boat a decision needs to be made about whether it is going to be put back to grow bigger or kept for a meal. If it's the latter then the fish should be dispatched as quickly and humanely as possible. Time to look for a priest – not the ones you find in a church, but a short weighted baton or length of wood. A couple of firm strikes to the back of the head should be enough to kill most fish, maybe a couple more for the bigger ones. It can be distressing if fish are left flapping about on deck, so using a priest as soon as the fish comes aboard is good for the fish and angler alike.

Some fish like turbot are bled by cutting across the wrist of the tail and hanging them up if space is available. This prevents the blood spreading to the flesh and leaves it nice and white. If pouting are to be cooked they should be gutted at once, as the stomach juices are very powerful and can affect the flesh. The fish should be put in a cool box as soon as they are caught if you want to maintain their freshness.

FILLETING

One of the first fish people catch is mackerel and they are an absolutely wonderful food if cooked really fresh. They are probably the easiest fish to catch, and it's certain that anyone reading this book will at some time catch several and wonder about eating them.

They can be cooked whole, which means just cutting off the head and removing the stomach contents. This is the best way when soused (see the recipe on page 172), but if they are to be fried or smoked this is how to fillet them leaving none of the fine bones (opposite). Removing the fine bones from the fillet can make all the difference to some people enjoying fish. Cut in close either side of the bones and lift the strip of flesh out with them.

With bigger fish such as cod the knife should first cut along the back, close to the dorsal fin, then work down easing the flesh off the back bone.

HOW TO FILLET A MACKEREL

Cut in just below the gill cover and always cut away from you.

Continue right to the tail with the knife, using the bone as a guide.

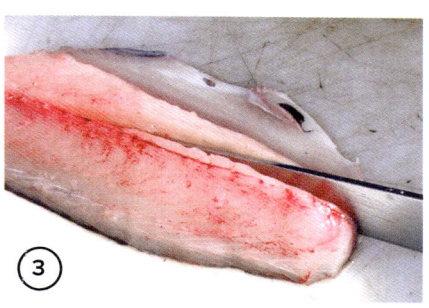

Turn the fillet skin-side down and feel for the fine row of bones. Make a cut either side.

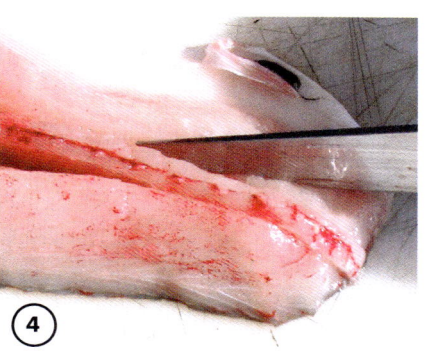

Cut away the strip of flesh containing the bones from the rest of the fillet.

FILLETING COD OR POLLACK

This method of filleting can be used for nearly all white fish.

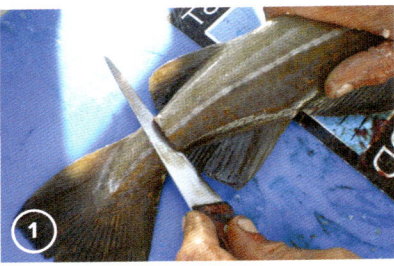

Cut across one side just above the tail.

Cut into the flesh and run the knife along the backbone.

Cut across the body just below the pectoral fin.

Gently work the knife parallel to the bone folding back the flesh as you go.

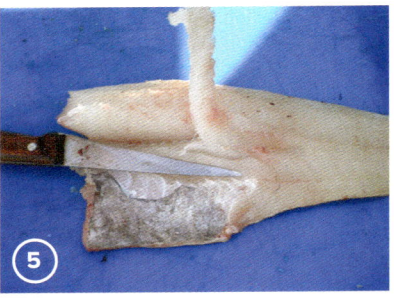

TOP TIP

Don't forget to remove the fine row of bones as on the left.

SKINNING

The skin can be removed from bream and bass very easily as it is very tough and easy to hold. Place the fillet with the flesh side uppermost. Ease the flesh off a little from the tail end with the knife and firmly grip the skin. Then slide the knife along between the skin and flesh, leaving it skin-free. Cod and pollack can be skinned the same way, but a little more care is needed as the skin is not so strong.

Note that cod and pollack can benefit from cooking with the skin on as this prevents the flesh from drying out and it holds the fish together.

READY TO COOK

Many children and adults are put off fish if they find skin or bones in it. The bream fillet pictured below has had both the skin and bones removed. It can now be used for frying, baking in tinfoil, microwaved, to make fish cakes, goujons or in a curry. Taking care to remove those fine bones is well worth the effort. We all know a healthy diet benefits from plenty of fish, and fresh fish, caught by yourself on rod and line, must be the ultimate feel-good food.

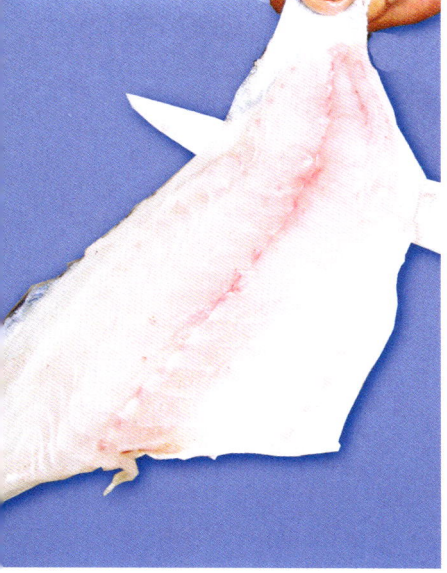
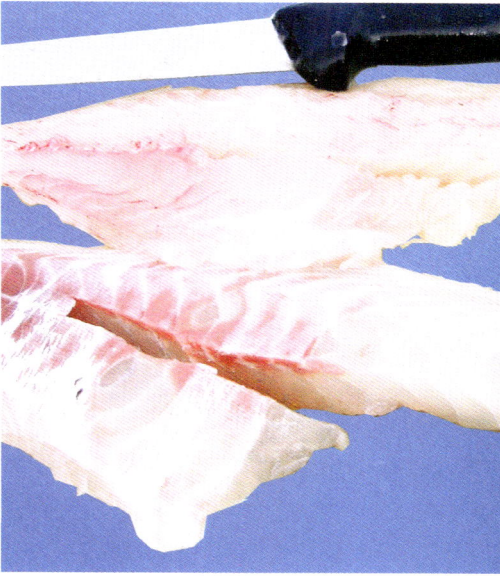

PREPARING OTHER TYPES OF FISH

Small plaice and dabs can be cooked whole after cutting off the head, tail and trimming the fins off with some kitchen scissors.

For medium-sized fish such as plaice, gut the fish straight after catching it by making a cut through the fish behind its head. To fillet, start with the white meat (the underside) as this is naturally thinner. Begin by slicing down the back as close to the backbone as possible and then slide the knife under the fillet and out to the side. Once the two fillets on the upper side have been removed, turn the fish over and repeat on the underside. This should give you four long, slim and completely boneless fillets.

Round fish such as cod, pollack, bream and mullet can be filleted by first cutting along the back either side of the dorsal fin from the head to the tail. This is best achieved by laying the fish on its side. Then work the knife into the cut and ease it down, freeing the flesh from the bone gently.

The garfish can be filleted into long strips or cooked whole, with the bones removed after the cooking process. Be warned – when cooked whole the bones will become a strange green colour, but this is not harmful.

⬆ Filleting a plaice by cutting down the centre and working under the fillet out to the side.

⬆ Cutting the fins of a small flatfish.

COOKING ON BOARD

The galley is an important part of the boat as there are no takeaways or fish and chip shops out at sea. Boats used by weekend sailors come in all shapes and sizes and most of them have at least some elementary form of cooking facilities on board. Others will have lavish equipment including ovens, microwaves, fridges and freezers, so we have given a spread of recipes to incorporate as many options as possible. The first picture shows a pretty well-equipped galley with ample space to store all the condiments, spices and sauces to create some interesting dishes.

The galley to the right is more like the basic setup found on the majority of small boats. It has two gas rings and a small oven beneath. But even with this limited equipment there's scope to cook most of the recipes shown. With a little imagination the recipe for oven cooking can be switched to poaching, and the small flatfish cooked in the microwave can be popped in the frying pan instead.

⬆ This galley is more basic, but well capable of producing the recipes in this book.

⬆ A well-equipped galley like this one can cope with most recipes.

LET'S GET COOKING

In this section are some simple recipes that can be made on board with limited cooking equipment. And at least one of these recipes can be fried, so there's something for everyone here. We have to presume there will be cooking oil and a few herbs and spices available to enhance the cooking process. Where anything different is required we have highlighted it. Everyone knows how to fry fish or pop a fish on the barbecue, so here are a few other simple ways to cook fresh fish. Most fish falls into family groups for cooking, so where a recipe is for cod it will be the same for pollack, while bass and bream can be treated the same way. These two are the only fish that need descaling if they are to be cooked whole. Most other fish can be skinned, although very often it's better to leave the skin on for cooking and remove it later.

WHOLE BAKED BASS

Bass are delicious to eat however they are cooked. The meat is firm and tasty and can be enjoyed equally with a stir fry or a salad, but is probably at its best when baked whole. If your boat has a cooker, then try it out. First catch a 2lb to 3lb bass (you are allowed to buy one if your angling skills let you down!) and cut off the fins with a sharp knife.

It's best to descale the fish outside as the scales can make quite a mess of the galley. Scrape a blunt knife, or use the back of a knife, from tail to head until all the scales are removed. If your oven is fairly small you may have to cut off the head too. Make a few cuts in the skin of the fish and season with salt, pepper and mixed herbs. Lay the fish on some tinfoil, cover with olive oil and wrap up in the tinfoil. Bake for 45 minutes at medium heat. When cooked, remove the foil gently and lift the fillets off the bone. Serve with salad and new potatoes.

SOUSED MACKEREL

This is a great way to use mackerel if you have caught too many to eat straight away. Sousing them means they can be eaten cold with a salad and they will last in the fridge for at least a couple of days after cooking.

Clean the mackerel and remove the head and tail.

Place in an ovenproof dish and cover the fish with one part vinegar to two parts water.

Soused mackerel can be served whole with a salad as shown here, or the bones can easily be removed by splitting open the fish and lifting out the backbone.

Add bay leaves, mixed spices, tomatoes, or whatever
is to hand to flavour. Bake for 30 to 40 minutes in a
medium oven (350°F, gas mark 4).

FISHCAKES

Most white fish can be used to make fishcakes, and the best of these includes fish such as cod, pollack, whiting and pouting. Fish such as bass and bream are better cooked whole or filleted, as they are a much firmer meat. Cook some potatoes until tender, mash them and keep them warm. The fish can be grilled for a few minutes before being flaked and added to the mashed potato. Mix in some butter, pepper and salt, then roll the mix into fishcake sized balls (below). It's best to chill these in the fridge for 15 minutes or so until they firm up. It makes them easier to cover firstly in flour, then a beaten egg mix and finally breadcrumbs. They need to be cooked in shallow fat for four to five minutes until golden brown – but they could also be drizzled in oil and oven-baked.

New potatoes garnished with herbs and some fresh salad leaves make a great accompaniment to these yummy fishcakes.

FLATFISH

Medium sized flatfish like plaice and brill are easy to deal with as they can be filleted. Very large ones like turbot can be cut into steaks, but it's the ones which are too small to fillet that people have trouble with. The best way to cook these fish – such as dabs and small plaice – is to cut off the head and tail, then using kitchen scissors, cut off the fins close to the body. Don't attempt to get the skin off as it will peel off easily after cooking, leaving a lovely white meat that can be eaten off the bone.

The best way to cook these small flatfish is in a microwave oven. Squeeze some lemon on them and leave a slice on top during cooking. They only need about three minutes and as they haven't had to be turned over they retain their shape. If frying is the only method available, it's best to cook them in batter to keep the fish from breaking up.

Once you have cooked your flatfish, serve it with fluffy white rice and vegetables of your choice. ➡

GOUJONS WITH CHILLI SAUCE

The great thing about goujons is that they can be made with any type of white fish; cod and pollack are the best bet. They can be served as a main meal or a buffet item and kids love them. Cut the fish fillets into thin strips 3cm wide by 12cm long, wash them off and dry them in kitchen roll. Cover the fillets in flour, dip them in a beaten egg and then cover with breadcrumbs. Fry them for a few minutes on either side until golden brown and serve with a chilli sauce dip.

These goujons are far superior to shop-bought fish fingers and your kids or guests will love them served with ketchup or a spicy chilli dip. ➔

BAKED COD OR BASS

When it comes to cooking a big cod it can be a bit daunting, as shop-bought cod is already filleted or cut into steaks. The best way to deal with it is to take off two large fillets. Cod is probably the best for frying in traditional breadcrumbs or batter, as it has a firm meat that doesn't fall apart when cooked. A large cod steak can also be baked in an oven as shown below. The fish stays nice and moist, and if cheese is not to your taste, flavour with lemon or tartare sauce.

Lay a fillet on tinfoil, splash on some olive oil and a touch of butter. Wrap up the fish in the foil and bake in a medium oven for around 30 minutes.

Open up the foil and put grated cheese on to the fish then grill for a couple of minutes until the cheese starts to brown.

Serve with some green vegetables and new potatoes and of course, a large glass of your favourite beverage.

Baked in tinfoil, the cod stays in good shape and the cheese makes it look rich. For those who don't like cheese, grill some tomatoes on top or use your imagination and add something to suit your taste.

Because fish is a fairly neutral flavour, it works well with things like shrimp and chilli sauce as well as the grated cheese shown opposite. →

FISH AND COCONUT CURRY

As long as you have a gas ring on the boat you can always make a fish curry. This recipe comes from Malaysia and can be adapted for most fish, but you will need to get ingredients like coconut milk, chillies, ginger and turmeric beforehand. Cut the fish into chunks and prepare any vegetables that are available (such as potatoes, carrots, squash, cauliflower or broccoli). Using a medium-sized saucepan add some olive oil, two crushed cloves of garlic, two finely chopped chillies and cook for a few minutes. Add a 400g tin of coconut milk, the fish and the vegetables. Bring to the boil and simmer for 10 minutes. To provide the eastern flavour add half a teaspoonful of turmeric, a dash of ginger, two teaspoons of soy sauce, a teaspoon of sugar and the juice from half a lemon. Allow this to simmer for another 10 to 15 minutes. Check that the vegetables are fully cooked before serving with a generous helping of rice and mango chutney.

PAN-SEARED COD OR POLLACK WITH TOMATO AND BASIL SAUCE

All large white fish such as cod and pollack can be used in this easy-to-prepare recipe. Basically it is fillets of fish shallow fried in either olive oil or butter and a tasty sauce of tomato and basil poured over the top.

SAUCE

Prepare the sauce by chopping tomatoes as small as possible, or use a blender if available on board. Add a little salt and pepper to taste, 2 tablespoons of butter and some fresh basil. If cooking for adults only, a splash of white wine will give it an added attraction.

FISH

Cook the fish fillets in a little oil or butter for about 5 minutes each side cn a medium heat until brown. If the fillets are thick they may need another minute or so. Remove the cooked fillets and keep warm. Now add the sauce to the pan and bring slowly to the boil. Simmer for a minute or so while serving the fillets and pour the sauce over the top for a very tasty meal.

⬆ Can be served with salad, rice or French fries, depending on the extent of cooking facilities on board.

RULES OF ANGLING

There are in fact very few rules an angler has to abide by, but there are a few unwritten ones, such as never get too close to another boat catching fish and certainly don't drive close to an anchored boat. Driving too close down tide to a boat on a drift could put the fish off and spoil the fisherman's day. In the UK no fishing licences are required for sea anglers, but there are a few restrictions to be aware of. Taking fish from one of the designated nursery areas is strictly prohibited. These areas are mainly estuaries and certain bays. There are around 40 areas in the country designated as nursery areas for bass. Most of these places are near nuclear plants and the rest are in tidal estuaries. Check with the local harbourmaster before you start fishing. It is also illegal to sell any fish caught unless you are in possession of a retail licence and you fish from a registered boat.

DEFINITIONS

An angler is someone who fishes for sport or for the pot, by fair and sporting means using a rod and line, and does not sell or barter part or all of his catch. A sea angler doesn't need a rod licence to fish from a boat providing he keeps to the rules. Charter skippers who take anglers out fishing must be licensed to carry passengers.

A fisherman is a professional who must fish from a licensed boat and be registered to catch fish by netting, potting, trawling and in some cases line fishing. The fish can then only be sold through a licensed retailer. They have to abide by strict quotas for some fish and must stick to rules about net sizes and number of days at sea.

SIZE LIMITS

Most fish can be kept for consumption provided they meet a minimum size limit. Commercial fishermen have a set of limits that are generally on the small side, so the national angling bodies have their own size limits. I would advise any casual angler to work to these sizes as well. A copy of the size limits is

available from the Angling Trust at www.anglingtrust.com. If these sizes are adhered to it means the fish are of a suitable size to eat, and if for some unlikely reason your fish were checked by a fisheries officer they would be comfortably within Government size limits. To be found with undersized fish is a criminal offence.

Make a point of putting back any fish not required for the pot and do it in a careful way so the fish can swim away safely. A fish thrown back carelessly would be easy prey to other species if it is stunned from the impact with the surface.

LOCAL LAWS

One of the biggest frustrations when moored in a harbour is to see big mullet swimming round the boat and not be allowed to fish for them. Some harbourmasters turn a blind eye to angling if it's done discreetly, but it's wise to check first if there are restrictions. Outside of the harbour, fishing will be allowed, but not in any of the deep water channels that have been kept dredged for large boats.

Fishing is fun and I hope with the help of the tips in this book you can not only enjoy your time afloat fishing, but will also catch some fresh fish to eat.

INDEX

Note: Headings in *italic* denote recipes and references in italic denote illustrations

INDEX